# Hey, God, What About . . . ?

# HEY, GOD, WHAT ABOUT...?

James T. Cumming
Hans Moll

Art by
Kathy Counts

Publishing House
St. Louis

Dedicated to the Glory of God.

7 8 9 10 11 12 MAL 90 89 88 87 86

Concordia Publishing House, St. Louis, Missouri
Copyright © 1977 Concordia Publishing House

MANUFACTURED IN THE UNITED STATES OF AMERICA

Library of Congress Cataloging in Publication Data

Cumming, James T 1938-
    Hey, God, what about ...?

    Includes index.
    1.—Theology—Miscellanea. I. Moll, Hans, 1938-      joint author. II. Title.
BR96.C85          230          77-9932
ISBN 0-570-03758-1

# Contents

# Preface

For our readers we ask "grace, mercy, and peace from God the Father and Christ Jesus our Lord" (1 Tim. 1:2). Amen.

Through the guidance of the Holy Spirit a question and answer book has been maintained in the main entrance to the Lutheran Student Center/Chapel of St. Timothy the Learner, Macomb, Illinois. This chapel serves the students of Western Illinois University. Students have been encouraged to ask, anonymously, questions that are of concern to them. These questions have all been carefully answered, after prayer, on the basis of the Bible and the Lutheran Confessions.

It was during the 1974 spring quarter that a student came to the campus pastor with a series of questions on Lutheran living and theology. In the course of helping this student search out and answer his questions, the student suggested that others had similar concerns, but lacked a convenient and private way of asking their questions. He further suggested that some way be provided so that others could benefit as he had. From these counseling sessions grew the question and answer book described above.

This book is based on the questions asked in the question and answer book. All of the questions in the volume are quotes from the original.

The purpose of this book is to spread the Gospel of Jesus Christ as it pertains to the daily lives of young adults living in the late 1970s.

The various questions and their answers can be organized into two major categories, Christian/Lutheran living and Christian/Lutheran theology.

All Bible passages quoted are from the Revised Standard Version (RSV) of the Bible, unless otherwise noted.

Thanks to Ed Higginbotham, who first proposed the question and answer book. Thanks also to the following people who encouraged us at various times during the preparation of the manuscript, Colleen Bellm, George and Phyllis Genseal, Arthur Kuehnert, Jan and Jerry Lindsay, Roger Loos, students at the Lutheran Student Center, the Mission Commission of the Central Illinois District of The Lutheran Church—Missouri Synod, and the Campus Co-workers Board. For typing we thank Phyllis Genseal and Linda Smith. Special thanks and love to wives Marcia and Margaret, and our children Amy, Carol, Christine, David, Debra, Emily, and Heidi for their support, encouragement, and understanding during the months of preparation and writing.

J. T. C.
H. G. M.

# ALPHABETICAL INDEX OF THE BOOKS
## OF OLD AND NEW TESTAMENTS

| Abbreviation | Book | Old Testament | New Testament |
|---|---|---|---|
| Acts | Acts | | X |
| Amos | Amos | X | |
| 1 Chr. | 1 Chronicles | X | |
| 2 Chr. | 2 Chronicles | X | |
| Col. | Colossians | | X |
| | | | |
| 1 Cor. | 1 Corinthians | | X |
| 2 Cor. | 2 Corinthians | | X |
| Dan. | Daniel | X | |
| Deut. | Deuteronomy | X | |
| Eccles. | Ecclesiastes | X | |
| | | | |
| Eph. | Ephesians | | X |
| Esther | Esther | X | |
| Ex. | Exodus | X | |
| Ezek. | Ezekiel | X | |
| Ezra | Ezra | X | |
| | | | |
| Gal. | Galatians | | X |
| Gen. | Genesis | X | |
| Hab. | Habakkuk | X | |
| Hag. | Haggai | X | |
| Heb. | Hebrews | | X |
| | | | |
| Hos. | Hosea | X | |
| Is. | Isaiah | X | |
| James | James | | X |
| Jer. | Jeremiah | X | |
| Job | Job | X | |
| | | | |
| Joel | Joel | X | |
| John | John | | X |
| 1 John | 1 John | | X |
| 2 John | 2 John | | X |
| 3 John | 3 John | | X |

| Abbrev. | Book | | |
|---|---|---|---|
| Jonah | Jonah | X | |
| Josh. | Joshua | X | |
| Jude | Jude | | X |
| Judg. | Judges | X | |
| 1 Kin. | 1 Kings | X | |
| 2 Kin. | 2 Kings | X | |
| Lam. | Lamentations | X | |
| Lev. | Leviticus | X | |
| Luke | Luke | | X |
| Mal. | Malachi | X | |
| Mark | Mark | | X |
| Matt. | Matthew | | X |
| Mic. | Micah | X | |
| Nah. | Nahum | X | |
| Neh. | Nehemiah | X | |
| Num. | Numbers | X | |
| Obad. | Obadiah | X | |
| 1 Pet. | 1 Peter | | X |
| 2 Pet. | 2 Peter | | X |
| Philem. | Philemon | | X |
| Phil. | Philippians | | X |
| Prov. | Proverbs | X | |
| Ps. | Psalms | X | |
| Rev. | Revelation | | X |
| Rom. | Romans | | X |
| Ruth | Ruth | X | |
| 1 Sam. | 1 Samuel | X | |
| 2 Sam. | 2 Samuel | X | |
| Song | Song of Solomon | X | |
| 1 Thess. | 1 Thessalonians | | X |
| 2 Thess. | 2 Thessalonians | | X |
| 1 Tim. | 1 Timothy | | X |
| 2 Tim. | 2 Timothy | | X |
| Titus | Titus | | X |
| Zech. | Zechariah | X | |
| Zeph. | Zephaniah | X | |

# Hey, God, What About ABORTION?

 **Q** *... if you had led your life in a wrong manner, such as sinning after you become a Christian, to a point where you're in a predicament such as abortion, how can you correct the situation if you can't get married and she can't have the baby?*

**A** When one puts his trust in Jesus, which is what becoming a Christian is, that does not mean that he never sins again. Rather sin is no longer his lord; Jesus is his Lord. Sin no longer has control of him (see Rom. 6:14), but Jesus does. This side of heaven the Christian is not perfect; he will fall into sin whenever he trusts in himself rather than in his Lord and Savior. The Christian is always in need of God's sustaining and renewing grace.

As the inevitable result of his sins of weakness, a man will find himself in many a predicament. He may have to endure the consequence of his sin, even though he would rather have matters some other way. Adultery or fornication is a sin; sin against the commandment which reads, "You shall not commit adultery" (Ex. 20:14). Conceiving a child is not a sin. One cannot "right" the consequences of adultery or fornication by destroying the already conceived child. Aborting the new life is a sin against another commandment, the one in Exodus 20:13: "You shall not kill." One sin can hardly undo another. Two wrongs do not make a right, because morals are not mathematical. Think about it. Via abortion you would be committing wrong against the only innocent party involved. Adultery or fornication might be called a sin of weakness, the weakness of the flesh, but deliberately taking the life of the prebirth child can hardly be considered the sin of weakness, but the sin of murder.

On the basis of Holy Scripture, I urge persons involved in the above situation to demonstrate that sin no longer has dominion over them by not compounding their present predicament by getting more deeply entangled in sin and its consequences. Do not let sin, even easy sin, have dominion over you.

Speak to those who will support you along the way. Seek out those who can show you that "she can't have the baby" is false. Marriage may not be the answer, but abortion on demand for your convenience is also not the answer. Talk to your pastor or such local prolife organization as Birthright; they are willing and able to help all *three* of you. If you do not wish to talk to someone you know, most prolife organizations are confidential. The essence of their help is love, and you know that true love does not destroy. Please let prolife Christians help you.

"Please, God, do not let sin have dominion over me. Please let Jesus be the Lord of my whole life. Amen."

# Hey, God, What About ATTENDANCE at Church?

 *What does the Bible say about attending a mass every week? I'm Catholic and never attend services. I don't think I need services to believe in God.*

To get a Catholic answer to this question you'll need to ask a Catholic priest. The answer that follows is a Lutheran answer given by a Lutheran pastor. This answer will not deal with Catholic mass attendance *per se.* It will give you what Lutherans say on the subject of worship, both public and private.

Worship is a response to what God has done for us. The most wonderful thing that God has done for us is send His only Son to bridge the gap between Himself and us. That gap is of our making. That gap is the result of our self-centeredness, our greed, our lust, our envy, etc., in other words, our sin. When we realize what a wonderful thing God has done for us in Christ Jesus, that is, freely forgiven all our sins and given us the gift of life with Him forever, we just can't stop worshiping, thanking, and praising him.

In private we praise God with prayer, Bible reading, thinking, and acting as we think God has told us to act.

Corporate worship is several people who have the same feeling toward God praising Him together. While it is true that each person believes *for* himself, he does not believe *by* himself. One of the reasons for attending worship service is to experience the joy of sharing a common faith with others who are in Christ. When you do such a thing you are building others up in their faith, while at the same time they are building you up in the Lord. That's what is called Christian fellowship; it happens when we worship together.

Since I believe that the Bible is the very Word of God, another purpose for attending service where the Word is preached is to hear what God has to say to me. It is only by hearing the Word of God that one comes to faith in Jesus, and it is only by continuing in His Word that one continues to be a disciple or follower of Jesus. One who cuts himself off from the Word of God will not remain a Christian. It is possible to know *about* God without the Bible, but it is only through the Bible that we *know* God. In the Bible and through the preaching of it we come to *know* a loving, forgiving, and faithful God in Jesus. When you really know such a God, worship is never a "drag."

Yes, you can be a nominal Christian and not go to church, but you cannot be a growing Christian without contact with other Christians. (See also the question on HOPELESSNESS.)

# Hey, God, What About BACKSLIDING?

**Q** *What is "backsliding" compared to a growing Christian?*

**A** At the outset it may be said that this question has a strange sound in Lutheran ears. We Lutherans do not speak very often of "backsliding." This seems to be the case because the Biblical terms and concepts for "backsliding" are found mostly in the Old Testament. The Hebrew words *sug, meshubah, shobab/shobeb*, and *sarar* are found in 17 places in the Old Testament, where they are translated as either "backsliding" or "backslider." Thirteen of these translations are found in Jeremiah, three in Hosea, and one in the Book of Proverbs. There is no exact counterpart in the New Testament Greek. Jesus Himself does not speak of backsliding or backsliders. The closest He comes to doing so is in Luke 9:62 when he says: "No one who puts his hand to the plow and *looks back* is fit for the kingdom of God."

In John 6:66 we also read: "From that time many of his disciples *went back* and walked no more with him" (KJV).

In Galatians 4:9 the apostle Paul chides his readers, who have known God, for returning to the weak and beggarly things to which they had once been enslaved.

Let's now look at what is involved in backsliding in the passages where the several Hebrew words are found: In Jeremiah 2:19 backsliding has to do with forsaking the Lord and not fearing the Lord; in Jeremiah 3:6 backsliding has to do with playing the harlot on every high mountain and under every green tree (translated into modern terms this means fornicating in pagan houses of prostitution); in Jeremiah 5:6-8 backsliding has to do with many transgressions, with the committing of adultery, with trooping to the harlot's house, and with neighing or lusting after the wife of one's neighbor; in Jeremiah 8:5-6 it has to do with holding deceit, with refusing to return to the Lord, and with turning into one's own way; in Jeremiah 49:4 it has to do with people glorying in their immorality.

Hence, this student of the Bible understands that the backslider is one who has known the grace of God, but who willingly has permitted sin to take dominion over him again. The backslider is one who trusts in himself and his sin rather than in Jesus. As his backsliding increases (Jer. 5:6), it has a snowballing effect in his life. In fact, we are told (in Jer. 14:7) that the sins of the backslider will testify against him. He will become filled with his wicked ways (Prov. 14:14). The sins of the backslider (Israel) are so bad in Jeremiah 3:8 that they lead to the divorce of the Lord Jehovah from His unfaithful wife. (In the Old Testament, Israel is pictured as the wife of God in the same way as the church is pictured as the Bride of Christ in the New Testament [Eph. 5:23-33].)

Yet, even for the backslider there is forgiveness with the Lord (Ps. 130:4). This is because the Lord is gracious and merciful, slow to anger and plenteous in mercy. He calls to His unfaithful wife to return to Him (Jer. 3:12, 14, 22). He promises to heal the backslider of his backsliding. He assures the returnee that His righteous wrath will not fall upon him. In Hosea 14:4 He indicates that He will heal the backslider and freely love him. He also says that He will feed the returnee as a shepherd feeds his lamb, that is, with tender loving care.

God's expressions of compassion work in the hearts of those who have fallen away. Listen to a prayer of confession found in the Book of Jeremiah:

"O Lord, though our iniquities testify against us, do Thou it [i.e., forgive us and save us] for Thy name's sake: for our backslidings are many; we have sinned against Thee." (Jer. 14:7 KJV)

Thus, we can say that, serious and damning as "backsliding" is, it is not something that cannot be reversed or forgiven. As long as the backslider is alive, he has a chance to come to know the mercy and the healing of the Lord again. What was true in Jeremiah's day is still true in our's. As long as there is human time, there is still room in the kingdom of God. No matter how far one has slid from the saving knowledge of God, Jesus the Good Shepherd seeks out the lost sheep. He is the only way that any sinner can come into the presence of the Father. It is only by putting one's trust in Jesus that backsliding can be reversed.

The opposite of backsliding is growing in grace and the knowledge of Christ. Spiritual growth takes place when one continues in Jesus' Word (John 8:31). One grows in Christ only when one puts his trust in Him alone and sinks his roots deeper and deeper into His Word. When one does that, the fruits of faith are produced in our lives. It is the Lord Himself who grants the increase; however, as we share our faith with others and they with us, we edify or build each other up in the Lord. We grow in Christ when we consciously do those things which we know are pleasing in God's sight and when we strive to imitate the examples Jesus and His servants have given us to follow. This side of heaven we cannot expect to attain perfection. In fact, the more we grow in Christ, the more we will realize how imperfect we are and how much we need the grace of God in Christ. We know we must trust in Him who is our Righteousness (Jer. 23:6). Praise God, to know Jesus is to know the Lord our Righteousness.

## Hey, God, What About BAD Times?

**Q** *I know in God's plan for my life there are bad times too, but how can I tell if it's the devil working or just my own evil self going against God?*

**A** You are right, as long as people are in this world there will be "bad times." Even when the Holy Spirit leads you to the realization that God loves you and that you are in His good hands, you will continue to have to contend with the devil, the world, and your evil self.

It is at times difficult to tell whether one is contending with the devil or with one's own evil nature. However, it is not absolutely necessary to make this distinction since the weapons God has given us work against both the devil and our evil selves.

Ephesians 6:10-20 tells us about the defenses that God has given us. These include the belt of truth, the breastplate of righteousness, the boots of the Gospel of peace, a shield of faith, and a helmet of salvation. The old evil foe, the devil, is shrewd enough to use both overt and covert attacks against those who belong to God. The Old Adam in us, our old evil selves, will use the same battle tactics. However, we are told that we will be able to stand against these combined forces when we are clothed in the armor of God described in Ephesians 6.

God has even given us an offensive weapon, the Sword of the Spirit or the Bible. With the Word of God we can attack the devil, the world, and our evil selves. As with any weapon, however, it is only useful when the user has been trained and the weapon maintained and used. Therefore, the Christian puts on the armor of God and practices with the Sword of the Spirit by reading the Bible, attending church and Bible class, and associating with other soldiers of the cross.

Ephesians 6 mentions the use of prayer as a weapon of the Christian, though it is not generally considered to be part of the God-supplied armor described above. Ephesians 6:18 urges us to pray and stay alert at all times in our struggle with the evil foe. We are to persevere and to be on our guard. Our prayers, however, are not only to be for ourselves but are to include all other people.

So, the identity of the enemy is less important than the struggle to overcome the devil, the world, and our evil selves. May God be with you in this earthly battle.

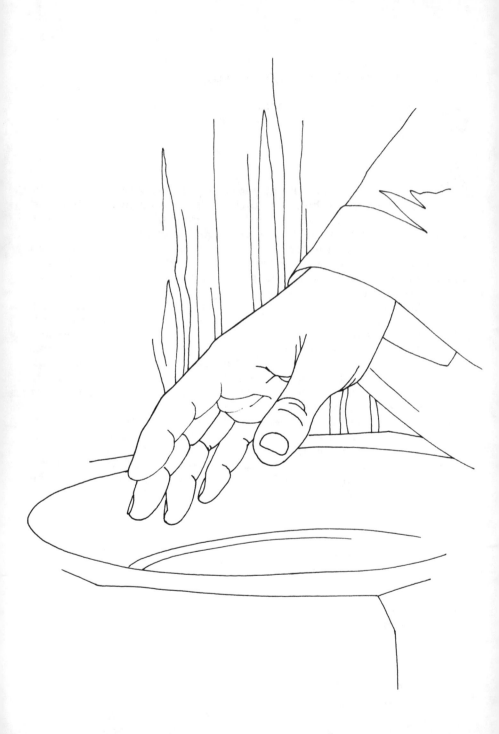

# Hey, God, What About BAPTISM?

**Q** *In Scripture, Baptism is always spoken of as burial (Rom. 6:4\*). It was always said that a lot of water was present before a Baptism took place. How then can you justify Baptism by sprinkling?*

*\* "Do you not know that all of us who have been baptized into Christ Jesus were baptized into His death? We were buried with Him by Baptism into death, so that as Christ was raised from the dead by the glory of the Father, we too might walk in newness of life." (Rom. 6:3-4)*

**A** Baptism is indeed spoken of as burial in this passage. It is also referred to as burial with Christ in Colossians 2:12\*\*. However, Galatians 3:26-27 says that in Baptism we put on Christ. In 1 Peter 3:21 Baptism is spoken of as a means of salvation. Therefore, Baptism is not "always" spoken of as burial.

Although alluding to a means of baptizing, Romans 6:3-4 *does not teach how* one is to be baptized, rather it teaches what happens when one is baptized. When one is baptized, he dies to sin (Rom. 6:2). He is joined with Christ in his death. He is also, however, joined with Christ in His resurrection. In Christ the baptized person walks in a new life. The meaning of Baptism, not the mode, is what God is telling us in Romans 6:3-4.

"To baptize" is "to wash." In Biblical times cups, pots, brazen vessels, tables, and couches were all baptized, that is, washed. You do not wash a cup and a table the same way. The way is not as important as the washing. That the washing is the important thing in Baptism is voiced by Ananias to Paul in Acts 22:16, when he said: "rise and be baptized, and wash away your sins, calling on His name." Note well that in the context of that passage nothing is said about how Paul was baptized.

You may also recall that in Acts 1:5 Jesus told His faithful ones that they would soon be baptized with the Holy Spirit. When that promise of both the Father and the Son was fulfilled (Acts 2), the apostles were not immersed in the lake or river of the Holy Spirit, but, rather, the Holy Spirit was *poured out upon* them. That is what Peter said in Acts 2:16-18:

"This is what was spoken by the prophet Joel: 'And in the last days
it shall be, God declares, that I will pour out my Spirit upon all
flesh, . . . I will pour out my Spirit; and they shall prophesy.'"

If God Himself can use "pouring out" as a means of baptizing, then those of us who do not insist on immersing in Baptism do not need to justify our procedure.

The question of procedure, however, is ultimately not the most

17

important one. The most important is whether you trust in Jesus as Savior and have been baptized for the remission of your sins. Do you believe in Jesus? Have you been baptized?

**The same New Testament Greek word, *sunthapto*, is used in both Colossians 2:12 and Romans 6:4. Another verb, *thapto* (the same root as the other), is used 11 times in the New Testament but does not refer to Baptism. In addition, the noun *baptisma* is found 22 times, the noun *baptismos* 4 times, the verb *baptizo* 74 times in the New Testament. So you see, being buried with Christ is only one of the ways in which Baptism is referred to in the Bible.

## Hey, God, What About the Necessity of BAPTISM?

**Q** *Is Baptism necessary for salvation? Why does God want us to be baptized?*

**A** All questions on Baptism, theology, and morals, must be answered by the Word of God, the Bible. In this case we will look at the words of Jesus and the statements recorded for us by his apostles in the New Testament.

In what is called the Great Commission, Jesus told His followers to go and make disciples by baptizing them in the name of the triune God *and* by teaching them to observe all things that He has commanded us (Matt. 28:19-20). Notice, Jesus does not say we *may* baptize. It is not a matter of choosing one of the two, teaching or baptizing. Both are necessary. The church has no choice where her Lord has spoken. In Mark 16:16 Jesus says: "He who believes *and* is baptized will be saved; but he who does not believe will be condemned." Notice the "*and*." From what Jesus tells us, both are necessary for salvation.

When Peter, on Pentecost, was filled with the Holy Spirit and preached his famous sermon, he really got through to his hearers. Acts 2:37 tells us that they were "cut to the heart" and asked the apostles what they were to do. Since they were moved to sorrow for what they had done to Jesus, the Christ, Peter told them:

"Repent, *and* be baptized every one of you in the name of Jesus Christ for the forgiveness of your sins; and you shall receive the gift of the Holy Spirit." (Acts 2:38)

Notice that in this reference there is again the "*and* be baptized." Just as Jesus stressed that it was necessary that one be born again "of water *and* the Spirit" (John 3:5) in order to enter the kingdom of God, so the apostles stressed the necessity of Baptism. Look at Acts 16 and you will see that, when Lydia and her household accepted the Word of God, Paul preached and that they were baptized (Acts 16:14-15). Also the jailor and his household believed in Jesus and they too were baptized (Acts 16:31-33). The necessity of Christian Baptism along with repenting/believing is found here and elsewhere in your Bible.

By way of exception to the rule, the thief on the cross at Calvary was saved by Jesus without Baptism. His was an eleventh-hour conversion. So, one can be saved by God without Baptism. But are you so sure of when you will die that you think you can wait till then to be forgiven?

Why does God want us to be baptized? In His conversation with Nicodemus, Jesus said, "That which is born of the flesh is flesh, and that which is born of the Spirit is spirit" (John 3:6). In order to enter the kingdom of God we must be born of the Spirit. It is interesting to note, as was done above, that this takes place when we are born again of "water and the Spirit" (John 3:5). What is this reference to the water but a reference to Baptism? Remember also what Peter preached about repenting and being baptized. In Acts 2:38 we are told that baptism is for the remission or the forgiveness of sins. Hence we can say that Baptism is for us a washing away of sins. If we have sins that need to be washed away, then we need Baptism. None other than the great apostle Paul was invited at the time of his conversion to "rise and be baptized, and wash away your sins" (Acts 22:16). That same apostle also writes to a young co-worker of the washing of regeneration and renewal of the Holy Spirit by which God in His mercy has saved us (Titus 3:5). What else can Paul be referring to but Christian Baptism? Look also at Ephesians 5:26 where Paul writes of Christ cleansing His church "by the washing of water with the Word." (See also the question about those who never hear of JESUS.)

## Hey, God, What About Different Types of BAPTISM?

**Q** *I've read that there are seven different types of baptisms mentioned in the Bible. What are these and what is their significance?*

**A** The following is a list of ways in which the word "baptism" is used in the Bible and in Bible times. The answerer does not claim that the list is complete. Use number six is the most important for today's Christian.

1. Secular usage: meaning simply "washing" or "to wash"
   —in Mark 7:4 the Greek noun *baptismos* is behind the translation "the *washing* of cups;"

—in Luke 11:38 the Pharisees marveled that Jesus did not *baptizo*, "wash," His hands before eating.

2. Ceremonial usage:
   —which is closely related to the secular usage;
   —it is identified with the purification rites of the Old Testament

3. Late Judaism's usage:
   —that is, the baptism of proselytes,
   —the rite of initiation for non-Jewish converts to Jehovah;
   —it was administered to "proselytes of righteousness" along with circumcision for the males.

4. John the Baptizer's usage:
   —which was preparatory for Jesus;
   —it was for all reached by his ministry (Mark 1:4);
   —it was a Baptism of repentance (Mark 1:4; Luke 3:3; Acts 19:4).

5. Jesus' Baptism by John:
   —found in Matthew 3:13-17;
   —it is unique, in a class by itself;
   —Jesus did not need Baptism for cleaning away of sin, since He is sinless;
   —He Himself said His Baptism was "to fulfill all righteousness."

6. Christian Baptism usage:
   —what Jesus commissioned His followers to do when making disciples for Him (Matt. 28:19);
   —this is the "one Baptism" of Ephesians 4:5;
   —it is for the remission of sin (Acts 2:38; 22:16);
   —it is God's means of grace to save and regenerate us (1 Pet. 3:21; Titus 3:5).

7. Figurative usages:
   7.1 by Jesus of what He was to experience, namely, His suffering and death (Matt. 20:22-23 KJV; Luke 12:50).
   7.2 by John and by Jesus of the coming of the Holy Spirit:
   —John said Jesus would baptize with the Holy Spirit (Luke 3:16);
   —Jesus said His disciples would be baptized
   with the Holy Spirit
   with power from on high
   as the promise of the Father (Acts 1:5);
   —such took place on Pentecost (Acts 2) and other times since then

8. Unusual (unclear) usages:
   —the baptism of the dead (1 Cor. 15:29);
   —the baptism of (into) Moses (1 Cor. 10:2).

## Hey, God, What About Interpreting the BIBLE?

 *Is it true that the Bible can be interpreted in so many different ways that it can fit everything I do?*

If your question is *can* such a thing be done, the answer is yes, because that is exactly what many people do with the Bible. These people read their own personal notions into what the Bible says, rather than let the Bible speak for itself. This misuse (abuse) of the Bible has been going on for a very long time.

However, if by your question you are asking whether the Bible *should* be interpreted in "many ways," that is an entirely different question. This student of the Scriptures is one who holds that it is not legitimate to twist the Bible's teachings to suit one's own fancies, to justify one's conduct or misconduct, or to support prevailing social notions. It is no more legitimate to do that to the Bible than it is to do that with what you are reading. The author's intention is to give you the most meaningful answer to your question. It is not proper for you to approach what we have written with the idea that it can mean anything you want it to mean. Certainly, you would not think it legitimate to apply whatever interpretation they wished to a letter you might send to your parents, your employer, etc. In order to understand a communication from someone else we must assume that the author of that communication had *one intended sense* in mind when he wrote or spoke the words he did. It is necessary for those of us on the receiving end of a communication to determine, by careful study, what the transmitter had in mind and intended to let us know. Usually communication between two contemporaries who are peers is not difficult. Contemporaries who are not peers have a little more difficulty communicating, e.g., you and your parents. When you read the Bible, you must realize that neither your contemporaries nor your peers are talking to you. You should also know that there is another factor that makes the communication difficult, namely that the English in the Bible is a translation of the Common Greek, the Hebrew, and the Aramaic of the original Bible. As a result, it takes careful study to determine what the *one intended sense* of a Bible passage is. Some passages of the Bible are not as hard to understand as others.

One assumption that we must make is that the authors of the Bible were honest and intelligent men who did not intend to deceive their readers, and that they had *one intended sense* in mind when they wrote. If you do that, I am sure that you will also come to the conviction that what you read in the Bible does not merely come to us from the hands of other

humans, but that the ultimate source of what you are reading is God Himself. And God's *chief intention* in inspiring the sacred writings we call the Bible is to make us "wise unto salvation through faith which is in Christ Jesus" (2 Tim. 3:15 KJV).

Since the Bible needs careful study to be understood, you should read some of it on a daily basis as part of your personal devotions. In addition, group study, as in Sunday school, Bible class, men's and women's study groups, etc. is a good way to get at the Bible's "one intention."

## Hey, God, What About BIBLICAL Contradictions?

*Doesn't it (the Bible) contradict itself in many ways?*

This question has been with the church for a long time. In *A Short Explanation of Dr. Martin Luther's Small Catechism* (1943) we find the following about the Bible.

Q. What is the Bible?

A. The Bible is the Word of God. . . .

Q. Who wrote the Bible?

A. Holy men of God wrote the Bible. The Prophets wrote the books of the Old Testament and the Evangelists and the Apostles wrote the books of the New Testament. . . . "Holy men of God spake as they were moved by the Holy Ghost" (2 Pet. 1:21 KJV).

Q. Why is the Bible the Word of God although it was written by men?

A. The Bible is the Word of God because these men wrote it by inspiration of God. "All Scripture is given by inspiration of God" (2 Tim. 3:16 KJV).

Q. What does "by inspiration of God" mean?

A. "By inspiration of God" means that God the Holy Ghost moved the holy men to write, and put into their minds, the very thoughts which they expressed and the very words which they wrote. . . . "We speak, not in the words which man's wisdom teacheth, but which the Holy Ghost teacheth" (1 Cor. 2:13 KJV).

Q. Whose word, then, is every word of the Bible?

A. Every word of the Bible is God's word, and therefore the Bible is *without error*. "Thy Word is truth" (John 17:17 KJV). . . . "The Scripture cannot be broken" (John 10:35 KJV).

We accept the above and, therefore, cannot accept the proposition that the Bible has even *one* error, much less many contradictions. We recognize that there are variant readings in the many manuscripts of the

Bible, that there are technical difficulties, and that there are differences of perspective, but we are not willing to admit that there are contradictions in the Bible.

If you have any specific concerns, any pastor can help you to understand the alleged contradictions. One such concern that has come to the attention of this pastor is the story of the paralytic healed and forgiven, Matthew 9:2-8, Mark 2:1-12, and Luke 5:18-26. As you read these accounts, you will find that they are not exactly the same. That, however, does not indicate that they contradict each other.

In Matthew we read that Jesus told the paralyzed man that he should "be of good cheer" (Matt. 9:2 KJV), whereas neither Mark nor Luke indicate that Jesus said that. The fact that neither Mark nor Luke included that expression in their accounts cannot be construed to mean that they deny that Jesus said such a thing. Surely, Jesus said much more than we find recorded in the Bible.

When we read these three accounts we find that the scribes and the Pharisees said to themselves similar yet slightly different things. Undoubtedly they did think the various thoughts recorded by the evangelists.

Q. For what purpose did God give us the Bible?

A. God gave us the Bible to make us "wise unto salvation through faith which is in Christ Jesus" (2 Tim. 3:15 KJV) and to train us in holy living. "Thy Word is a lamp unto my feet and a light unto my path" (Ps. 119:105 KJV).

"O God, help me to read the Bible so that I too can be made 'wise unto salvation.' In Jesus' name. Amen."

## Hey, God, What About BIRTH Control?

**Q**  *Does the Bible say anything towards birth control?*

**A**  In 20th-century terms the Bible does not have much to say about birth control. Except for *coitus interruptus*, the Bible does not seem to refer to this subject.

However, the Bible does have a great deal to say about the related subjects of the sanctity of human life, marriage, and sex. What the Bible says on these matters helps a person make decisions in the area of birth control. As with sex itself, so there is a proper use as well as an improper use of birth control.

To start with we read in Genesis 1 that the Lord God *blessed* and commissioned the first human couple to be fruitful and multiply. Hence the Christian does not consider children "accidents" but blessings. He considers children to be the natural fruit of the union of one man and one woman in holy matrimony. From a Biblical point of view procreation is considered one of the purposes of marriage.

In Genesis 2 we find the second and closely related purpose of marriage. There God said, "It is not good that the man should be alone; I will make him a helper fit for him" (Gen. 2:18). And that is what God did; he provided a companion for man. Companionship is the other basic purpose in God's design for marriage and the proper use of sex. Sexual intercourse is one of the expressions of love, respect, and commitment that a man and a woman feel toward each other. Since there are only a few days each month that a couple can conceive a child, and since God does not tell us in His Word that we should only engage in sexual intercourse on those fertile days, procreation (reproduction) cannot be said to be the only reason God ordained sex. When we realize that, we can say that there is a proper use of birth control in marriage.

That said, one realizes that birth control can be abused. It is abused when it is used by those who are not married. Extramarital sex is called adultery and fornication and is condemned everywhere in the Bible as abuse of the God-given gift of sex. Using "the pill" or other means of birth control to prevent the conception of an out-of-wedlock child does not justify it or make fornication any less sinful.

When abortion is used as birth control, it must be recognized for what it is, namely, taking the life of an individual human being. The convenience of the mother or father can hardly be invoked as justification for the destruction of another human being.


## Hey, God, What About Being BORN Again?

**Q** *How do you get born again?*

**A** One is born again by water and the Spirit, which is to say that God causes man to be recycled in His image. We do not cause ourselves to be born again, anymore than we cause our own physical conception and birth. Physically, we are conceived and born by the act of man and woman. Spiritually, it is by an act of God that a sinner is born again.

In James 1:18 we read, "Of His own will He brought us forth by the Word of truth." The original word for "brought forth" was normally used with regard to what a mother did when she gave birth to the baby or babies she was carrying. In Luke 2:7 (KJV) we read the very familiar "and she brought forth her firstborn son, and wrapped him in swaddling clothes."

In the context of James 1:18, it is God who is said to cause our rebirth. Note that it is by the Word of truth that this takes place. The Word of truth, as indicated in other passages in the New Testament, is one of the ways of referring to the Gospel. It is the Gospel that is the power of God unto our salvation. In other words, the message of the Gospel has the power of God to convert the sinner from his sin to God. It is by hearing and accepting God's message of Jesus and His love that God causes us to be born again.

On our side we can speak of receiving Christ (John 1:12) and of believing in Him (Acts 16:31, 34) but even that receiving is the work of God the Holy Spirit in our hearts (John 3:6; 1 Cor. 12:3). It is absolutely necessary for the Holy Spirit to create faith in our hearts, because by nature we are blind to the things of God (1 Cor. 2:14); we are dead in our trespasses and sins (Eph. 2:1); and we are enemies of God (Rom. 8:7). There is simply NO WAY we could bring about our own regeneration.

The one way of our rebirth is by the will and grace of God. We who know His good will and His amazing grace know that we cannot praise Him enough for our salvation. (See also the questions on PREDESTINATION and FAITH.)

## Hey, God, What About When I CAN'T Stop?

**Q** *What do you do when a guy you really love and you make love and you kind of go a bit further than you want to, and even though you know you shouldn't you still do no matter how hard you try? Also I can't stop until it grosses me out. Help!*

Your question sounds much like the person who wrote:
"I do not do the good I want, but the evil I do not want is what I do. . . . Wretched man that I am! Who will deliver me from this body of death?" (Rom. 7:19, 24).

You are a person who is "under the power of sin" (Rom. 3:9). You are letting sin reign in your body so that you are obeying its passions (Rom. 6:12, 19). You have yielded the members of your body as instruments of impurity.

Those are hard words, but they need to be spoken to you. You are confusing love and lust. According to God's design for the use of sex "the body is not for fornication" (1 Cor. 6:13 KJV; *porneia* is the Greek word for fornication here). According to God's design, sex is to be used within the bonds of holy matrimony as an expression of the lifelong commitment that husband and wife have made to each other. Any other use is an abuse of a powerful and beautiful gift of God. Your conscience bothers you

26

because you have sinned against God, against yourself, and against him who may some day be your husband.

The questioner needs to ask herself if she is being used by the other person. Admittedly our sex drive is very strong, but is the questioner really ready to say she cannot stop, cannot say "NO." Do you think that you are a mere animal who when in heat, "has no choice"? What is in charge? Your mind, or your emotions?

Paul answered the question he asked in Romans 7:19 and 24, about who would deliver him, with the words, "Thanks be to God through Jesus Christ our Lord" (Rom. 7:25). Jesus Christ is the Deliverer. He is the One who delivers us from all sin, including lust and fornication. Jesus, the Deliverer, is also the One who "helps us free from every need that hath us now o'ertaken." Seek the forgiveness and the help that Jesus alone can give though prayer. Talk to your minister who will keep your confidence and can work with you to overcome the power of the flesh.

## Hey, God, What About CHARISMA?

**Q** *What are the spiritual gifts? I have heard that speaking in tongues is the least important (maybe wrong word) of them? How do you receive these gifts?*

**A** "Spiritual gift(s)" is the English translation of the New Testament Greek words *charisma, charismati,* and *charismata,* which are found in several places in the original text of the New Testament. There are *seventeen* places where one of these three related words is found. In *ten* places, the text and the context do not specify what the gifts mentioned are. In *three* places, the gift of God is clearly our salvation in Christ Jesus and, therefore, is synonymous with the simpler word *charis* or "grace." *Charisma* is used in this way in Romans 5:15-16 and Romans 6:23. In *four* places, all of which are in one chapter of the Bible (1 Cor. 12), *charisma* definitely refers to extraordinary gifts of the Holy Spirit. Hence, most of the time, i.e., 13 out of 17 times, *charisma,* etc. does not refer to anything extraordinary.

In 1 Corinthians 12:4 *charismata* is translated as "gifts" in the Revised Standard Version. In 1 Corinthians 12:9 *charismata* is associated with healing; the phrase is translated as "gifts of healing" in the RSV. The same phrase is in 1 Corinthians 12:28. In 1 Corinthians 12:31 we are urged to earnestly desire the "higher gifts."

In 1 Corinthians 12 "speaking in tongues" appears eighth in a series of nine manifestations of the Spirit (1 Cor. 12:8-10). "Tongues" appear last in a list of eight gifts in 1 Corinthians 12:28. In these two lists you can see that utterance of wisdom, of knowledge, of faith, the working of miracles and prophesy, as well as teachers and healers are listed ahead of "tongues." This answerer would, therefore, conclude that "speaking in tongues" is indeed the least important of the spiritual gifts.

What can one do to receive spiritual gifts? Wait for the Giver to give them to you. Grace or *charis* is a gift of God, one that is given without any merit or worthiness in us. God's grace in Christ is not given to us because we deserve it in any way, but because we need it in every way. You cannot do anything to get the grace of God. He gives it to us freely in Jesus. God's grace is His *charis*. The *charisma* or *charismata* (which could be called "gifts of grace" as well as "spiritual gifts") are also freely given by God to His people. It appears that each person does not get all the gifts of God, but God distributes them as He sees fit (1 Cor. 1:7).

"Waiting on the Lord" is another way of speaking of trusting in God. If you trust in Jesus for the forgiveness of all your sins and for the gift of eternal life, then also trust Him to give you what you need to serve Him now. He never fails, for with that trust you have the spiritual gifts you need. (See also the question on "TONGUES")


## Hey, God, What About COMMUNION Preparation?

*Pastor, in confirmation class as a child I learned that Communion could be taken to your damnation. To avoid this, I understood a Christian should "examine" himself, namely, look at his sinfulness, read over Luther's Christian Questions and their answers.*

*At times I have come to church and have forgotten that this was a Communion Sunday. I have not "contemplated" my sins until I sat down in church and saw the Communion cup on the altar. I have wondered then, have I examined myself sitting there in church, or should I not take Communion and wait until the next time when I won't be caught unprepared?*

*Was this not the church's intention a few years ago when it was required to register for Communion in church the week before, or to stop and see the pastor to register during the week?*

You have a very valid concern, and it is based on the teaching and practice of Holy Communion as given us in 1 Corinthians 11:23-29. The apostle Paul gives his account of the institution of the Lord's Supper, and then comments on it. In his commentary he tells us that it is possible to eat and drink "judgment" ("damnation" KJV) when one does not discern the Real Presence of Jesus' body and blood in Holy Communion.

The doctrine of the Real Presence is clearly taught in 1 Corinthians 11:27, where Paul tells us that he who eats and drinks the bread and the cup of the Lord in an "unworthy manner" ("unworthily" KJV) will be guilty of profaning not bread and wine but "the body and blood of the

Lord." 1 Corinthians 11:28 tells us that in order not to profane the Lord's body and blood and not eat and drink judgment upon ourselves we are to "examine" ourselves.

In Lutheran practice it is expected that each person be instructed in basic Christian doctrine before communing. Such instruction includes the fundamental teaching of the Bible that all people are by nature and action sinners before God, as well as the message of the cross, which declares us righteous before God for Jesus' sake. Included in instruction preparatory to participation in the Lord's Supper in our circles is the teaching and the acceptance of the conviction that Jesus' body and blood are truly present "in, with, and under" the bread and wine in the Sacrament. The instruction also includes the Biblical directive (1 Cor. 11:28) that each time we plan to attend the Lord's Supper we consciously examine ourselves. By examining ourselves we first review our conduct according to the standard of the Ten Commandments; second, see whether we are truly sorry for our sins; and third, resolve, with the help of God, to amend our sinful ways. Dr. Luther offered his "Christian Questions" to help people prepare for Communion. Those questions and answers are a concise presentation of why we need the grace of God in Christ as well as a winsome reminder of how, in both Word and Sacrament, God has so graciously provided for that need.

The practice of announcement before the Communion celebration is a fine practice that has regretfully fallen into general disuse in our circles. It seems to have been a practice that did not survive our denomination's transition from a rural to an urban setting. It was a good custom, intended to motivate people to make preparation for attendance at the Lord's Table. It was designed to make people prepare for Communion before they arrived at worship on the day that the Sacrament was celebrated.

This pastor does not attend the Lord's Supper on the "spur of the moment." He will not attend Communion on a Sunday or at a place where he did not realize beforehand that it was being offered. He offers this same advice to those instructed for membership in our midst. Such advice is given so that each communicant may enjoy the benefit (i.e., the assurance of forgiveness and the strengthening of faith) that the Real Presence of Christ in the Lord's Supper has to offer. There is a real blessing to be enjoyed by those who have prepared themselves, and you know that we humans can use all the real blessings we can get.

# Hey, God, What About CREATION and Christ?

**Q** *What does Revelation 3:14\*, where Christ is referred to as the "beginning of God's creation," mean? Christ wasn't created, so what does it mean?*
*\*"The words of the Amen, the faithful and true witness, the beginning of God's creation" (Rev. 3:14).*

**A** You are correct when you state that Jesus was not created. Clear passages in the Bible tell us that Jesus is God. He is eternal, that is, without beginning or end. Jesus is called the Son of God, but that does not mean that there was a time when He was not. When we call Jesus the Son of God, or God the Son, we are speaking of His relationship to the Father within God's triune nature. Thus, Revelation 3:14 cannot mean that Jesus was the first *thing* that God created.

Had you read the New International Version rather than either the King James Version or the Revised Standard Version you may not have even had the question. The NIV reads: ". . . These are the words of the Amen, the faithful and true witness, the ruler of God's creation." That this is a clearer translation you will see from what follows.

First, look at Colossians 1:15-18. There you will find, in verse 18, that Jesus is called "the beginning." The same New Testament Greek word, *arche*, is found in Colossians 1:18 as in Revelation 3:14. In the Colossians text Jesus is called many other related titles. He is said to be the Head of the Church. He is said to be before all things, and all things hold together in Him. In and through Jesus all things are said to have been created. He is also said to be the image (visible form) of the invisible God, and the firstborn of all creation. In this section of the Word of God the contrast between Jesus and created things is obvious. Yet, Jesus does have a relationship to created things. They are made through Him. They had their beginning in Him and they are under Him. Colossians 1:18 indicates that the meaning of *arche* is ruler or chief. This meaning would also apply to Revelation 3:14.

Second, in Revelation 1:5 Jesus is referred to as "the faithful witness... and the ruler of the kings of the earth." In the original Greek, the word is *archon*, which is closely related to *arche*. In verse 8 Jesus calls Himself "the Alpha and the Omega." Verses 17-18 give us a further explanation of what that means, as Jesus tell us that He is "the first and the last, the living one." The word "first" is *protos*. It is found several times in Colossians 1:15-18, mentioned earlier. The expression "the first and the last" is found not only in the Book of Revelation but also in Isaiah 41:4, 44:6, and 48:12, where it is used by the Lord Jehovah of Himself. Hence, Revelation 1 identifies Jesus with God. As God is First, so Jesus is First, or the Eternal Number One.

Third, John 1:1-3, 14 tells us that the Word (Jesus) was God, as well as with God, and that all things were made through Him. That of course is the same idea as expressed by the apostle Paul in Colossians 1.

Hence, it can be said that Revelation 3:14 does not teach that Jesus is the first thing that God created. Rather it teaches that all things came into being through Jesus. He was the Beginner, and therefore He is the chief, the ruler, and the head of all created things.

## Hey, God, What About Being CURSED Forever?

 *Who is any man that does not have God in his heart and is loved by man? Let him be the devil and cursed forever.*

You are correct. Man is by nature cursed forever. Man is by nature dead in his trespasses and sins (Eph. 2:1).

You are wrong. God alone judges and as such we cannot tell if a man is cursed forever. For by the grace of God, through the work of the Holy Spirit, we can have Jesus in our heart and can be saved.

> Jesus sinners doth receive;
> Oh, may all this saying ponder
> Who in sins delusions live
> And from God and heaven wander!
> Here is hope for all who grieve—
> Jesus sinners doth receive.
>
> Oh, how blest it is to know:
> Were as scarlet my transgression,
> It shall be as white as snow
> By Thy blood and bitter Passion;
> For these words I now believe:
> Jesus sinners doth receive.
>
> Jesus sinners doth receive.
> Also I have been forgiven;
> And when I this earth must leave,
> I shall find an open heaven.
> Dying, still to him I cleave—
> Jesus sinners doth receive.

*The Lutheran Hymnal,* 324:1, 6, 8

# Hey, God, What About DATING?

 *How can I tell for sure whether or not the Lord wants me to be dating a particular guy? I can't say for sure he isn't Christian or is Christian.*

You must arrive at an answer to your question based on your experiences while dating the particular guy. If the things that you do together are pleasing to the Lord, then you can be sure that God would approve of your dating the guy. Conversely, if the things you do together are displeasing to God, then you can be sure that He does not approve. What God has revealed in His holy law, the third use of the Law, is a sure guide for us to follow in our relationships with people of both sexes. In other words, don't expect God to approve of anything that is contrary to His revealed will.

In the dating relationship you would certainly want the relationship to be one of respect, trust, and mutual upbuilding. As Christians we do not use or exploit those whom we date.

Before you get seriously involved with another person in the dating and courtship process, you should be certain of his Christian faith or lack of it. Peter says that we are to be "joint (i.e., husband and wife) heirs of the grace of life" (1 Pet. 3:7). Because of this beautiful "joint heirs" image the apostle Paul warns the Christians that they should not be "mismated with unbelievers" (2 Cor. 6:14).

Now, how do you go about getting the information? If you are starting to get serious about each other, you should be talking about many things that are of interest to each of you. Since you are a Christian, your spiritual life is important to you, and anything that is important to you should also be important to him. Ask him what he thinks about spiritual matters.

Ask him, for example, what he thinks of Jesus. Ask him if he is sure, that if he died tonight, he would go to heaven. Ask him what he would say to God if he were asked why he should be permitted to enter God's heaven. Questions like these get right to the heart of essential spiritual matters. Such questions keep us from getting sidetracked into likes and dislikes about church buildings, church services, particular ministers, and other religious hang-ups and ax grinding.

Our prayer for you is the first verse of the wedding hymn of one of the answerers.

> Blest be the tie that binds
> Our hearts in Christian love;
> The fellowship of kindred minds
> Is like to that above.

*The Lutheran Hymnal, 464:1*

## Hey, God, What About Being DRAWN to Church?

 **Q** *HELP! I'm lost. I don't know what I'm doing. There's something that drew me here. What is it? Help!*

**A** The Holy Spirit has drawn you to this chapel so that you can become acquainted with Jesus.

Jesus said that He came to seek and to save the *lost*. He is looking for you. It is now a matter of your meeting Him. The only way you can meet Him is through the Bible. So we suggest you start by reading the Bible every day (we suggest the Gospel of St. John first). As you read, you will have questions. There are several ways to go about getting answers.

One way is to also read a catechism. A catechism is a series of questions and Bible based answers, much like this book. *Luther's Small Catechism* deals with the chief parts of Christian doctrine and would be very helpful.

A second way to answer questions and begin to find your way is to attend church on a regular basis. Here you can talk about your feelings and continue to learn about Jesus.

Third, you can visit with a pastor on a counseling basis or join an information class on the teachings of a church.

As Christians we believe Jesus is THE ONE WAY. When you have Jesus you are on the correct way and will no longer feel lost, since Jesus, the Good Shepherd, will have *found* you.

Begin finding your way right now by praying this prayer:

"I am weak, but You are mighty. Help me, O my God! Amen."

## Hey, God, What About EDIFICATION?

 **Q** *In 1 Corinthians 14:4\* the word edifies is used. What is the Greek meaning for this word? What does it mean to edify oneself? Is the meaning different for edifying oneself as compared to edifying the church?*

**A** *\*"He who speaks in a tongue edifies himself, but he who prophesies edifies the church" (1 Cor. 14:4).*

The word that is translated "edifies" in the Revised Standard Version of 1 Corinthians 14:4 is, in the Greek original, a form of the verb, *oikodomeo*. The exact same form of *oikodomeo* is found twice in that verse. Hence, the verb for edifying oneself is the same as the verb for edifying the church. What is of special interest is that this verse is the only verse in the New Testament that uses *oikodomeo* in a self-centered way. There are, by contrast, many places in the New Testament where *oikodomeo* is used for something we are to do for others. In 1 Corinthians 14:4 one edifies oneself when one speaks in tongues, whereas one edifies the church when one speaks prophecy.

The Greek word for edify can be and is translated as "to build," "to build up," and "to embolden." The noun form, *oikodome*, is found in numerous places in the New Testament and is translated "building," "edification," "edifying," and "edifies." In 1 Corinthians 14:3 the noun is rendered "upbuilding" in the RSV and "edification" in the KJV. The noun form is also found in vv. 5 and 12 of the same chapter. In 1 Corinthians 14:3 we are told that "upbuilding" is the purpose of speaking in prophecy. In verse 5 the church is edified when one speaks in prophecy and when there is an interpretation of tongues, and in verse 12 the readers are urged to excel in "building up" the church.

The noun form of *edify* is also found in three verses of 2 Corinthians (10:8; 12:19; 13:10), three verses of Ephesians (4:12, 16, 29) and two verses of Romans (14:19, 15:2).

The verb form of *edify* is found in Matthew 7:24, 26; 26:61; Mark 14:58; 1 Corinthians 8:1, 10; 1 Thessalonians 5:11; 1 Peter 2:5.

When one reads these passages of God's Word, one is impressed with the fact that when we are "in Christ" we are not "turned in" to ourselves but lose ourselves in service to others. We serve by building them up (i.e., edifying them) in Christ.


## Hey, God, What About FAITH?

**Q** *Does God determine your faith?*

**A** The brevity of this question makes it difficult to be certain that we understand what you are really asking. The key word, however, is faith, which in the New Testament means *trust*.

Thus to believe in God does not merely mean to believe in His existence; it means to put one's trust in Him. Believing or having faith in Jesus is to trust in Him for the forgiveness of all our sins and for the gift of eternal life.

In our relationship with other human beings, we only trust those people who have demonstrated their trustworthiness. So it is with our relationship with God. He has demonstrated His trustworthiness by sending His only Son, Jesus, to die on a cross for our sins. In response to this gift we trust in him to save us from our sins.

Personal faith in Jesus is expressed by confessing Jesus as Lord. We only make such a confession of faith when the Holy Spirit has been at work in our hearts. Jesus even said that no one comes unto Him unless the Father draws him, (John 6:44) and that it is the Father in heaven who reveals the truth about Himself to us. (See 1 Cor. 12:3; Matt. 16:17.)

One must always remember what man is before he is brought to faith in Jesus. According to the Holy Scripture man is spiritually blind to the things of God (1 Cor. 2:11, 14), he is dead in trespasses and sins (Eph. 2:1-5), and he is an enemy of God (Rom. 8:7). We by nature cannot turn to God; we need to be turned, we need to be converted, we need to be born again. The gracious God and Father of our Lord Jesus Christ does just that for us, through the work of the Holy Spirit, and that is why we give *all* glory to God.

Hence, with the understanding that faith is a trust response to the grace of God, and that such a trust response is the very work of the Holy Spirit within us, it is possible to answer "Yes, God does determine our faith." (See also the questions on PREDESTINATION and AND BORN.)

## Hey, God, What About the One True FAITH?

**Q** *How are you certain that this church is the one true faith to believe in?*

**A** One ought to be certain that the congregation and the association of congregations of which one is a member is teaching the truth. Since God is the source of all truth, it is from God alone that we derive the ultimate answer to the question of whether the church (congregation and/or denomination) one belongs to teaches the one true faith. God Himself has given us a revelation of His grace and of the propositional truths about many things in His Holy Word. Jesus Himself says of the Bible: "Thy Word is truth" (John 17:17). So what a church teaches should only be evaluated against what God has told us in the Bible. The Bible is the standard that we are to use in determining whether any teaching of any church is the one true faith or not.

This book is derived from the ministry of a group of Christians which confesses the Bible as the only source and norm for Christian faith and life (in this case, members of The Lutheran Church—Missouri Synod). We believe the Bible, in all its parts, to be the very Word of God. And we believe that our teaching is in accord with the teachings of the Bible. We invite all who are interested to investigate and ask about our teachings and how they square with the teachings of the Bible. It is the purpose of "this book" to make people wise unto their salvation through faith in Christ Jesus. We propose to do that by writing that which is given to us by inspiration of God in the Bible (2 Tim. 3:15-16).

Understand that when we claim to teach the one true faith, we do not mean that there is no one else who teaches of Jesus and His love. Many others do, and we thank God that is so.

Specific questions about The Lutheran Church—Missouri Synod can be asked of any Missouri Synod minister.

## Hey, God, What About FALSE Prophets?

*In the New Testament there are many prophecies about false prophets. If a person thought he might be one by his own life situation compared to the teachings in the Bible, how could he change his destiny, if it is destiny? 2 Peter 2:1-2\**

*\*But false prophets also arose among the people, just as there will be false teachers among you, who will secretly bring in destructive heresies, even denying the Master who bought them, bringing upon themselves swift destruction. And many will follow their licentiousness, and because of them the way of truth will be reviled. (2 Pet. 2:1-2)*

There are indeed many prophecies in the New Testament about false prophets. Because there are so many it is not always easy to determine which person fulfills a specific prophecy. What one needs to do with a particular prophecy is to look at what the false prophet teaches and/or denies. The standard they are measured against is, of course, what God has revealed to us in the Bible.

In 2 Peter 2:1-2 the false prophets mentioned are those who work in secret. As such, they would not walk around telling people they are false prophets. They would, however, deny the Lord who bought them; which means that they would not confess that Jesus paid for all their sins by shedding His blood on the cross. They would deny that they belong to Him. Because of these denials, they will bring destruction upon themselves; which means that they will get what they deserve for their sins, namely eternal death.

The destiny of those who teach and live under the dominion of false doctrine is not destiny, it is the natural result of their sins. That natural consequence of sin will only be changed when the person casts himself upon Jesus. Jesus is the Way to the *destination* of eternal life, the opposite of eternal death. Jesus is the Way even for the person who has been a false prophet. All he asks is repentance and faith.

Today Thy mercy calls us
To wash away our sin.

However great our trespass,
Whatever we have been,
However long from mercy
Our hearts have turned away,
Thy precious blood can cleanse us
And make us white today.

*The Lutheran Hymnal,* 279:1

## Hey, God, What About My FEELING Lost?

**Q** *I feel like a lost soul. What should I do?*

**A** It is to seek and to save the *lost* that Jesus came. He is the Good Shepherd who searches diligently until he finds the one lost sheep out of a flock of 100 (Luke 15:3-7). Jesus is searching for you.

He will find you when you recognize that your sinfulness and your sins are the cause of your lostness. He will find you when you are ready to trust in Him as your only deliverer.

Anyone who is a member of the flock of the Good Shepherd will be happy to help you learn to trust in Jesus. From the Bible you can learn to know Jesus as well as learn how to serve Him. (See also the question on being DRAWN to church.)

## Hey, God, What About My FEELING Toward You?

**Q** *Is God a loving, forgiving being or is he someone to fear?*

**A** In Jesus Christ I know God as my merciful Father. Jesus not only talked about God's love, He demonstrated it by humbling Himself and becoming obedient unto death on the cross. On the cross Jesus suffered and died for my sins and for the sins of all people. I know that I do not deserve the love of God, but by the working of the Holy Spirit in my heart I know that I need that love. The Holy Spirit bears witness in my heart that I am a child of God. By His gracious working I know

39

that I have been adopted by God's grace into His family. Yes, you and I can *love* God because He first loved us.

The man or woman who is in Christ does not fear God in the sense of being afraid that His wrath (anger) will fall upon him. On the cross Jesus bore the wrath of God for the sins of all people. Hence, because of Jesus, the believer in Jesus is no longer under the condemnation of the law of God. In Jesus sin and death no longer have donimion over us. As long as we put our trust in Jesus we do not need to fear God or His wrath. But remember, there is another side to that coin. The person who does not trust in Jesus for forgiveness and life, trusts in himself. The opposite of being in Christ is being *in sin*. The person who lives in sin will die in sin. He is already under the wrath of God, under the condemnation of the Law. Such a person has reason to fear God.

However, there is a sense in which even the person who loves God "fears" Him. In that meaning of fear we reverence and stand in awe of God, because He is almighty, majestic, glorious, eternal, holy, etc. and of course we are none of these things. It is with a mixture of this kind of fear and love that the believer in Jesus worships God. Such fear is good, for it does not have the guilty-conscience aspect that the fear under-the-wrath-of-God outside-of-Christ has.

I pray that you too will love and fear God and trust in Him above all things. In Jesus' name. Amen.


## Hey, God, What About FORGIVENESS?

*God, forgive me, please.*

"There is forgiveness with [the Lord]" (Ps. 130:4).

"If anyone does sin, we have an advocate with the Father, Jesus Christ the Righteous" (1 John 2:1).

"If we say we have no sin, we deceive ourselves, and the truth is not in us. If we confess our sins, He if faithful and just, and will forgive our sins and cleanse us from all unrighteousness" (1 John 1:8-9).

So says the Lord God in His holy Word, the Bible. Therefore, you can be certain that your sincere request for forgiveness will be given the positive answer: "Your sins are forgiven."

## Hey, God, What About FORGIVING Others?

 **Q** *In the Lord's Prayer we pray, "Forgive us our trespasses as we forgive those who trespass against us." Since our forgiveness is by no means so perfect as God's are we placing limits on His forgiveness by the amount that we forgive? Perhaps we should pray the Lord's Prayer as "forgive us our trespasses as we should and try to forgive those who trespass against us."*

**A** You make interesting comments on a very common expression. It is good to know that some people take what they say in the Lord's Prayer seriously. Certainly we should not think of the Fifth Petition of the Lord's Prayer as placing limits on God's forgiveness. His forgiveness in Christ is full and free. However, in your statement you suggest changing the words Jesus gave us in His model prayer. Therefore your question is not an easy one.

First, permit me to state something we Lutherans usually memorize in Junior Confirmation Instruction, that is, Luther's meaning to the Fifth Petition. It goes: "We pray in this petition that our Father in heaven would not look upon our sins, nor on their account deny our prayer; for we are worthy of none of the things for which we pray, neither have we deserved them; but that He would grant them all to us by grace; for we daily sin much and indeed deserve nothing but punishment. So will we also heartily forgive, and readily do good to, those who sin against us." Note that in his meaning Dr. Luther places the emphasis on what we are to do and why.

Second, Jesus in the Fifth Petition of His Prayer has given us words to pray which fit together with the rest of what He has taught us in the gospels about forgiveness. In fact, immediately after the giving of the model prayer, Jesus said:

> "For if you forgive men their trespasses,
> your heavenly Father also will forgive you;
> but if you do not forgive men their trespasses,
> neither will your Father forgive your trespasses."

(Matt. 6:14-15)

Our forgiveness and our forgiving go hand-in-hand. Our attitude toward why and how we have been forgiven and why and how we forgive others go together. If we think that God forgives us because we deserve to be forgiven or because we have done something to merit His favor, then we are liable to think that someone else will need to deserve or earn forgiveness from us. Jesus' words do not teach us to think that we can limit God's forgiveness; they admonish us to think properly (i.e., Biblically) about both our forgiveness and our forgiving.

Third, Jesus even told a parable about an unforgiving servant. You'll find it recorded in Matthew 18:23-35. In that parable the unforgiving servant is in debt to the king to the tune of $10,000.00; and when he is asked to pay up he is unable to do so. And so, he, his wife, and his children were ordered to be sold into slavery in order that the debt might be paid. But the servant falls down before the king and pleads that he be given time to pay his debt. Instead of giving him the time he asked for, the king, moved with pity for the man, erases his debt completely. The king, at his own expense, forgives his servant. That's pure grace. Upon his release the forgiven servant finds a fellow servant who was in debt to him. After his experience with the forgiving king you would think that he, the forgiven servant, would also be a forgiving servant. But he is not; we call him the unforgiving servant. Instead of forgiving, he demands payment from his fellow servant. The fellow servant only owed him $20.00. This second servant pleads for time, much the way the first servant pleaded with the king, but to no avail. The second servant was put in the debtors prison until the $20.00 debt could be paid off. Now when the forgiving king heard what the man he had forgiven had done to one of his own, the first servant was summoned to appear before the king again. This time he was reprimanded and thrown into the debtors prison; he lost his forgiveness, and would spend a long time in prison working off his $10,000.00 debt. Jesus closes his parable with the words,

"So also my heavenly Father will do to everyone of you, if you do not forgive your brother from your heart" (Matt. 18:35).

In conclusion, I would agree with you that our forgiving is in no way as perfect as God's, but when we pray as Jesus taught us in the Lord's Prayer we should be aware that we must forgive others as freely as God in Christ has forgiven us. This pastor does not think that in the Fifth Petition we limit God. Rather, he feels that in this petition we are placing an obligation upon ourselves. That said, we must pray for a full measure of God's Spirit so that we will think, and strive to do (forgive) what we know is pleasing to God. Such thinking and doing can begin with the Fifth Petition of the Lord's Prayer.

## Hey, God, What About My GUILT?

**Q** *After leading a life of immorality and lust, can a person be forgiven, even though it may have been pathological. How do you shake the guilt?*

**A** Sin is always pathological. Sinning by immorality and lust may give you some "kicks," but sin will always kick you back in the end.

Sinning may give you some laughs, but sin has the last laugh. Yes, sinning is pathological because sin kills. The apostle Paul said the same thing when he wrote: "The wages of sin is death" (Rom. 6:23).

Guilt is another result of sinful, immoral, and lustful conduct. Guilt is real. Don't let anyone talk you into thinking that guilt is merely psychological. There is more to guilt than just a feeling. Even people who try to deny the reality of sin feel guilty because they know they *are* guilty. The only answer, the only way to resolve guilt, is to find real forgiveness.

One must do more than recognize one's guilt. One must feel sorry about it. One must feel real and deep remorse over the evil one has done against others, oneself, and God. That sorrow is not the sorrow of getting caught. That real godly sorrow will move the person to repentance (2 Cor. 7:10). Real repentance will move the sinner to humble himself and to plead for forgiveness from those whom he has offended. That plea cannot be made with any mental reservation. The plea of the repentant sinner is simply made because the pleader knows that he needs, really needs, the forgiveness for which he asks. He knows that he is guilty and he knows he needs mercy, not justice. He will address those whom he has offended and say to God the words the publican in the temple used: "God, be merciful to me a sinner" (Luke 18:13).

As Jesus taught in that parable, the man who humbled himself before God "went down to his house justified" (Luke 18:14). So there is forgiveness with the Lord (Ps. 130:4) for every repentant sinner.

Only the Law half of Romans 6:23 was quoted above. The Gospel or Good News half continues with ". . . But the free gift of God is eternal life in Christ Jesus our Lord."

God so loved the world, which is full of us poor, miserable sinners, that He did something about sin. He sent His only Son into this world. During His life and especially in His suffering and death, Jesus took all the guilt and all the kickbacks, and all the last laughs, and all the wages of all sin of all men upon Himself. On the cross Jesus took our place. Jesus willingly gave His life for us. And *in* Jesus real forgiveness and real freedom from guilt is to be found. In Jesus there is real life. Jesus alone is the answer to real guilt. Jesus alone is the One who can resolve real guilt. No sin (with the exception of the sin against the Holy Spirit (Matt. 12:31-32) is so bad that God will not forgive it. His mercy endures forever (Ps. 136:1).

The unlimited mercy and real forgiveness of the Lord is ours for the asking. All *anyone* needs to do is accept what and whom God offers. "What" God offers is full and free forgiveness of all sin. "Whom" He offers is His Son, Jesus. There is forgiveness *in* Jesus. The person who is *in* Jesus is one who grows in the realization of how wonderful it is not to live in fear of God but in His love. When one knows that God loves him in spite of his sin, one feels the love of God in his heart and the guilty feeling will be shaken. When one learns that God really forgives *all* our sins then the guilt feelings will go.

In the Bible we read that many members of the body of Christ were

44

great sinners. King David was guilty of lust, immorality (in his case, adultery), lying, and complicity in murder, yet he found there was forgiveness with the Lord (Ps. 51 and 130). A man named Levi was a traitor to God's people. He cheated them, and yet Jesus called Him with the simple words: "Follow me" (Matt. 8:22). Levi became Saint Matthew the apostle and evangelist. Remember also that Saul of Tarsus, who consented to the stoning of the first Christian martyr, became Saint Paul the apostle. God not only forgives sinners; He makes saints out of them. He can make a saint out of you.

## Hey, God, What About HARASSING Others?

*I want to know if it is natural to have an urge to harass people. I don't intend to injure one's feelings. It just seems to make me accepted by my peers.*

According to the Bible's description of humans as self-centered, the urge to "put others down" would be natural. Natural, however, is not always good.

We all like to be accepted by our peers. In order to gain that acceptance we often *conform* to the conduct of those around us. Such conforming can include involvement in activities and attitudes that bother our consciences. And even if such involvement does not bother our consciences, it may still be contrary to what God has revealed to us in the Bible as pleasing to Him.

God is certainly not pleased with attitudes and activities that "put down" other people. He wants us to love, help, and build up others. Jesus speaks of the person who is the greatest in the kingdom of God as the one who serves the most. Jesus Himself even took upon Himself the form of a servant. He came to serve us. He would have us serve each other. He would have us even be subject to each other because we love Him. He wants us to love our neighbor as we love ourselves. All of this is quite the opposite of harassing others.

Instead of *conforming* to this world (one's peers) the apostle Paul urges us to be *transformed* by the renewal of our minds. Only Jesus can renew us. Only Jesus can give us new minds. When you appreciate the fact that God lavished His mercies upon you in Christ Jesus, you will want to present your body as a living sacrifice to God (Rom. 12:1-2). God does not need the sacrifice of a flower, a fruit, or an animal. He does not need us either, but we need Him. When we give ourselves to Him, He renews and transforms us, so that we do not want to conform to the many and varied negative things that our peers expect of us. The person who is in Christ wants to do what pleases God. The person who is in Christ wants his thoughts and actions to be acceptable to God. Trusting in the mercy of God, he strives to do just that.

> Oh, that the Lord would guide my ways
> To keep His statutes still!
> Oh, that my God would grant me grace
> To know and do His will!
>
> Assist my soul, too apt to stray,
> A stricter watch to keep;
> And should I e'er forget Thy way,
> Restore Thy wandering sheep.

*The Lutheran Hymnal*, 416:1, 3

## Hey, God, What About HOMICIDE?

**Q** *What does the Bible say about patri-, matri-, sui-cide? Is it ever allowed?*

**A** Killing one's father, one's mother and/or oneself all fall under the prohibition of the commandment of God: "You shall not kill" (Ex. 20:13).

The person who looks to the Bible for guidance from God in matters of life and death could never think that God would *allow* or be pleased with such acts of homicide. (See also the question on SUICIDE.)

# Hey, God, What About HOMOSEXUALITY?

*How come the church is still down on homosexuality?*

*In 1961 Illinois was the first state that dropped laws against private sex acts between consenting adults, many states have also followed this move to allow sexual freedom between people of the same sex. Psychiatry Diagnostic and Statistical Manual (DSM), which used to include homosexuality on its list of abnormal behavior has recently dropped it out of its sexual deviation category and now looks at homosexuality as a normal variant of human sexual behavior. Since the world is now recognizing that homosexuality can be healthy for the emotional stability of its participants and the gay crowd is not infringing on society's heterosexual majority, why then does the church condemn it?*

*Did you know that the University of Texas, Austin, during the 1974—75 academic year allowed a homosexual club to be organized as an official organization on campus? And that even included a faculty advisor, which was necessary to have to become an official campus organization.*

*How long will the church preach against homosexuality?*

**A**

Christians who still take the Bible seriously are "still down" on homosexuality because according to the Word of God the only proper use of sex is between a man and a woman who are joined together in one flesh in holy matrimony. Sex outside of marriage is condemned by God. He condemns fornication, adultery, homosexuality, lesbianism, and bisexual activity. These deviations from God's norm are defined as follows:

1. fornication:
    a. is used in the broad sense to include all sexual intercourse between members of the opposite sexes who are not married to each other; in this sense fornication includes adultery;
    b. is also used in the narrower sense and is applied to sexual intercourse by unmarried persons of the opposite sexes;
2. adultery:
    a. is used to refer to sexual intercourse between members of the opposite sexes who are married, but not to each other;
    b. is also used more generally to apply to all explicit sexual intercourse by persons of the opposite sexes which is outside of wedlock; in this sense adultery includes fornication;
3. homosexual activity:
    a. is used in the broad sense to include all explicit sexual activity by members of the same sex; in this sense it includes sodomy (male and male) and lesbianism (female and female);

    b. is also used in the narrower sense and is applied to explicit sexual activity by two or more males;

    c. the term "gay" is slang used to refer to persons and activities of persons of homosexual persuasion:

4. lesbian activity:

is used to refer to the explicit sexual activities between two women; hence, lesbians are female homosexuals;

5. bisexual activity:

is used to describe activities of persons who are neither exclusively heterosexual nor exclusively homosexual.

The use of sex outside of marriage by members of the opposite sexes or members of the same (*homo*) sex is clearly condemned by God in the Bible. Homosexual conduct is condemned as unnatural and sinful in Romans 1:26-27. It is one of the sins that has resulted from men and women turning from God (Rom. 1:21; 26-27). God condemns as abomination (i.e., perversion) a man lying with another man as he would with a woman, as well a man dressing or giving the appearance of being a woman (Lev. 18:22; Deut. 22:5). The tragic history of the once-great cities of Sodom and Gomorrah is the classic example of the sexual perversions of mankind and the condemnation of God that befalls those who participate in them. Read about Sodom and Gomorrah in Genesis 13:13, 18:16-23 and 19:1-29. Since the time of Sodom and its destruction the perversion of sex engaged in between two males has been called sodomy. The perversion of sex engaged in between two females is called lesbianism; this expression comes to us from ancient Greece, not the Bible. On the Aegean isle of Lesbos a woman by the name of Sappho was said to have sexually enticed other women with her love lyrics. Additional references to homosexual behavior are found in 1 Timothy 1:10 where homosexual behavior is cited as an example of sin, and in 1 Corinthians 6:9-10, where it is regarded as a sin that makes one an unrighteous person who cannot inherit the kingdom of God.

All of the above must be taken into consideration to understand why the church which tries to speak God's Word faithfully is "still down" on homosexuality. In such a church, God's law is used as a curb against the coarsest outbreaks of sin, as a mirror to reveal our sin and need for forgiveness, and as a rule to guide the Christian to live in a God-pleasing way. In such a church the Gospel is also spoken to those who sin. The Gospel is the great Good News that there is forgiveness for *all* sins in Christ Jesus. All sins include homosexual conduct, because such conduct is not the unforgivable sin.

Implied in your question is the concept that that which the world considers alright should be accepted by the church. There are many in our world who have accepted the antiphilosophy that teaches that there are no absolutes and that therefore all things, especially morals, are relative. Against such a background it is not surprising that so many people "opt" for what Francis Schaeffer calls "statistical morality." In "statistical morality" when enough people do something, then that activity is considered acceptable. That is the way it is today in many areas of contemporary living.

However, do you really think that the church, which is called both the body of Christ and the bride of Christ, should go along with moral relativism and statistical immorality? Do you think that Christians, who know what God says about the use and abuse of sex, will simply conform to the unstandards of our world? Consider this:

"I appeal to you therefore, brethren, by the mercies of God, to present your *bodies* as a living sacrifice, holy and acceptable to God. . . . *Do not be conformed* to this world, but *be transformed* by the renewal of your mind" (Rom. 12:1-2).

You ask, "How long will the church preach against homosexuality?" We answer, "As long as it is faithful to the Word of God."

## Hey, God, What About My HOPELESSNESS?

**Q** *My older sister is a member of The First Church of God and many times she has said that my fiancee and I are hopeless because we do not faithfully attend services—although we are strong believers. I realize how important it is to attend services. However, what is your view on such a devout Christian saying that we are hopeless cases? She says according to the Bible certain churches (Catholic in particular) go against God's Word. What is the Lutheran view on this?*

*Also on her belief that a good number of the churches don't preach salvation and the members of these churches will not go to heaven. I was confirmed Lutheran (Missouri Synod) and whenever someone says I may as well be a Catholic I wonder— from what facts do they draw this belief.*

You have asked several questions that we will answer in the same order in which you asked them.

Faith in God (which is trust in Jesus) is not static; it is dynamic. It never stays the same. It either gets weaker or it grows stronger. The only way for one's faith to grow stronger is to feed it. We can feed our faith with the spiritual food that God offers us. The basic spiritual food—soul-food, if you will—that God offers us is His Holy Word. Jesus tells us that we must continue in His Word if we are to continue to be His disciples (John 8:31). It may be that your sister is trying to tell you that you cannot rely on what your faith was. To trust in Jesus as Savior and Lord is to live in Him day by day. When we live each day "in Christ" then worshiping regularly with others who have the same trust is not a chore, it is a joy. Joining with other Christians to sing God's praises and to hear His Word

49

is not an "I have to" thing, it is an "I want to" pleasure. (See also the question on ATTENDANCE at church.)

Personally, I don't think anybody is a "hopeless case." Jesus is the Hope of the world. He wants all to know His love and to really live by faith in Him. It is possible that your sister is being supercritical of you and your fiancee because of some spiritual laziness and complacency that she perceives in you. With her strong words she may be trying to joggle your conscience. If the shoe fits, wear it.

One must be careful when one criticizes others. Blanket indictments are at least unwise. We believe, teach, and confess that only those who trust in Jesus for the forgiveness of all their sins are now saved and will go to heaven if they continue in that faith. The grace of God for our salvation is an absolutely free gift. If individuals, congregations, or denominations do not teach this chief article of the Christian faith, they are indeed not Christian. In addition, when we believe that the Bible is the very Word of God we know that it is the final norm against which the teachings of churches are to be judged. We must be critical of any teaching which is contrary to what is taught in the Bible and especially of teachings that lead people to trust in themselves rather than the work of Christ in their behalf. Such teaching is to be labeled false doctrine. Hence, on specific teachings, specific denominations are found to be lacking from a Biblical point of view.

The assertion that "Lutheran is just like Catholic" is an inept judgment that some people voice. It is an assertion made on the basis of the observation that in certain externals Lutheranism and Roman Catholicism are similar. We both use altars and crosses in our church buildings. We both use regular orders of worship. Lutheran pastors and Roman Catholic priests wear robes when leading worship, and some Lutheran pastors wear clergy collars. Both the Lutheran Church and the Roman Catholic Church baptize the children and we both use the rite of confirmation and speak of the Sacraments (we count only two, however). But Lutherans and Roman Catholics are not the only churches which have these things in common. My advice is to ask the next person who makes the above assertion to be specific about what they mean.

## Hey, God, What About INTERRACIAL Marriage?

**Q** *Does the Bible say anything about interracial marriage? Also, what are your views on interracial dating?*

 **A** You will not find the word "race" in reference to skin color in the King James Version of the Bible.

In Genesis 10:5, 20, and 31 you can read that divisions among men are according to tongues, families, nations, and lands. In Revelation 7:9 (KJV) the redeemed of God are said to have come from "all nations, and kindreds, and people, and tongues." The Bible does not speak of divisions among men according to the color of their skin. In fact, Acts 17:26 reads: "From the one man He created all races of men" (TEV).

My personal opinion is that there is nothing morally wrong with interracial marriage or dating. That, however, does not mean that I do not see numerous problems. The couple should not kid themselves into thinking that *they* will have no problems. Society itself will give them problems. The couple must also examine why they are dating or wish to be married. Marriage is tough enough without marrying for the wrong reasons. One must also consider that when two individuals marry, the two families are also joined. Much conversation and much airing of feelings between family members should take place before such a marriage.

In the Old Testament there are prohibitions against Jews marrying non-Jews. Even in the New Testament those who trust in Jesus are told not to be joined in marriage to unbelievers (2 Cor. 6:14). Such a prohibition for Christians is given for many reasons (see also the question on DATING). But 2 Corinthians 6:14 should not be used to forbid the marriage of a man and woman who are both in Christ, but whose skin color happens to be different.

## Hey, God, Is JESUS a Myth?

**Q** *What is your opinion on those who believe Christ is a myth or a legend made up by some writer or novelist? Was Christ really a Jew?*

**A** The idea that a writer or a novelist made up the character of Jesus of Nazareth seems a bit farfetched, since there are at last nine different early followers who wrote about Him in what is now called the New Testament. In addition to those first followers of Jesus, countless others who do not put their trust in Him, and even oppose Him, have written about Him. In fact, Muhammad spoke of Jesus. Muhammad and his Muslim followers do not deny the existence of Jesus of Nazareth, but they do not accept His basic teaching about Himself, namely, that He is the very image of the invisible God. Most Jews do not deny Jesus' existence either, but it is obvious that they do not accept Him as their Messiah.

What we do know of Jesus comes to us primarily through the writings of the New Testament. But you might wonder—how reliable are these writings? Well, there are only 250—300 years between the events recorded in the New Testament and the earliest complete copies of the New Testament. The earliest surviving copies of seven plays by Sophocles are from 1,400 years after his death. With the writings of Euripides there is an interval of 1,600 years. With the writings of Plato the earliest document is from 1,300 years after the famous philosopher himself. (See F. G. Kenyon, *Handbook to Textual Criticism of the Bible*, p. 5.) Modern man does not deny, much less seriously question, the historicity of these men, If we accept secular writings removed from their events by more than 1,000 years, how can we deny religious writings dated much closer to their events?

Was Jesus a Jew?

The genealogy of Jesus given in Matthew 1 starts with Abraham, the first Jew, and comes down to Joseph, the husband of Mary. Joseph was Jesus' legal father and stepfather. Later in Matthew 1 we read that Joseph was convinced that the child which Mary was carrying was not conceived by fornication. Jesus was indeed the "seed" (*sperma* in the Greek) of the Virgin Mary, and Mary, like Joseph, was a Jew, according to Luke 1. Jesus then could hardly have been anything but a Jew.

But the most important question is not academic; it is very personal. That question is: "What do *you* think of Jesus?" Your destiny in this life and in that which comes after death depends on what you think of Him.

## Hey, God, What About Those Who Never Hear of JESUS?

*What is your opinion on salvation for those who have never been baptized Christians and/or those who have never heard of Christ?*

My convictions on these questions are dictated by the teachings of Holy Scripture. In order to answer in a meaningful way, your question must be divided into two parts.

First, concerning those who have never heard of Christ, I believe, with the apostle Paul, that "they are without excuse" (Rom. 1:20). Since God makes Himself known through the things that He has made, and since those things have been declaring His glory ever since their creation no one can say "I did not have a chance to know God." All people are also responsible before God for their actions. Yet, all people are under the power of sin (Rom. 3:9); "none is righteous, no, not one" (Rom. 3:10); all fall short of the glory of God (Rom. 3:23).

Understand that the person who has not heard of Jesus and His love is not judged for not hearing of Him. One is judged on the basis of what one has done with one's natural knowledge of God. Romans 1 tells us what people by nature do with the truth about God as revealed in the creation. It tells us that they, in their wickedness, suppress it (Rom. 1:18). They turn God's truth into a lie and worship and serve the creature rather than the Creator (Rom. 1:25 and 23).

God does not find the heathen guilty according to a standard they never knew. Romans 2:12 tells us that those who have sinned without having the Law (the Ten Commandments are its summary) will perish without the Law. The law they shall be judged by is written in their hearts. The wages of all sin is death (Rom. 6:23).

Any sin brings the payment of death, while by contrast God gives the gift of eternal life to all men in Jesus (Rom. 6:23). If people could be saved without knowing Jesus, then Jesus would not be the only way unto the Father (John 14:6). If people can be saved without hearing of Jesus and His love, then there would be no real motivation for evangelism or world mission work. In fact, if one says actively rejecting Christ is the only way that one is damned then why should missionaries go to the heathen and spoil their chances of being saved through ignorance of Christ as their Savior?

The Christian is one who has learned from the Bible that faith in Jesus comes *only* by the hearing of the Word of God, by hearing the message of the cross. (Rom. 10:17). The Christian also is aware of the obligation to share the message of Christ with as many as possible. This is done directly by witnessing to relatives, friends, and neighbors and indirectly through supporting the work of others in other places. The Christian knows he is his brother's keeper.

Second, concerning being saved without being baptized, it is inconceivable to this answerer how anyone who really has put his trust in Jesus would not want to be baptized in His name. It is possible, like the thief on the cross, to be saved without being baptized, but who wants to take such a chance with eternity? Augustine is reputed to have said "It is not so much the lack of Baptism that damns, but the despising of it." For one who believes in Jesus there will simply be no question that he will be baptized. He will surely want to enjoy all the blessings God offers him.

Permit me to add a few words about the perennial question about what happens to babies who die without being baptized. Those of us who have committed ourselves to teach only what the Bible teaches are not able to invent a place like limbo to answer this nagging question. To Christian parents we offer the comfort that God hears the prayers that we speak to Him in behalf of our prebirth children. Since children *en utero* are very much alive (ask an expectant mother!) parents can certainly intercede for them on behalf of their physical and spiritual welfare (which includes the forgiveness of sin). We can do so with the confidence that God hears the prayers of his people. Such a child might die without the benefit of Baptism, but he need not die without the benefit of the fervent or strong prayers of a righteous parent (James 5:16). (See also the question about the necessity of BAPTISM.)

# Hey, God, What About JESUS' Blood Brothers

**Q**

*Pastor, did Jesus have any blood brothers born of His mother after his own birth?*

This pastor believes that Jesus had brothers and sisters who were born to His mother, the Virgin Mary. Such a conviction is based on the following:

1. The literal, simplest meaning of the New Testament Greek word *adelphos* (masculine) is *brother* and of *adelphe* (feminine) is *sister*. Jesus' mother and His brothers came to see Him while He was preaching (Matt. 12:46). The residents of Nazareth spoke of Jesus, Mary, His brothers (James, Joseph, Simon, and Judas) and his sisters (not named) (Matt. 13:55-56). In the second text the original words for brother and sister mentioned above, are both used. In Galatians 1:19 the apostle Paul mentions that he saw James, brother of the Lord.

2. If these brothers of Jesus were not Mary's children, then why is it that they always seem to be mentioned with her? Note that in the Matthew 12 text Jesus' brothers are mentioned as being with Mary. Note also that in the Matthew 13 text the people who are with Mary are called Jesus' brothers and sisters. Even after Jesus' resurrection from the dead, Mary and "his brothers" are mentioned as being numbered among the disciples (Acts 1:14).

Now, it must be admitted that Jesus, as well as the Scriptures, and the church have used the term "brother" and "sister" to refer to those who were not blood brothers/sisters of Jesus. The term brother is used of those who are members of God's family via grace. In Matthew 12:50 Jesus uses the broader sense of the word brother. You'll find this use also elsewhere in the Bible, but that does not contradict the literal sense of the word as found in Matthew 12 and 13.

Those who think that Mary did not have any other children after Jesus, maintain that she remained *semper virgo* ("always virgin"). They say that those who are called Jesus' brothers and sisters were his cousins or other close relatives. It is possible to think of the *adelphos* and *adelphe* mentioned with Mary as Jesus' cousins, but that is not the simplest explanation of those texts. Lutheran Bible study says that the simplest explanation of a text is often the best. In this case the suggestion of some meaning other than brothers and sisters requires one to give further explanation. For instance, why are these people *always* with Mary? We believe that *semper virgo* is a traditional and extra-Biblical view and, as such, need not be accepted.

## Hey, God, What About JESUS Christ?

**Q** *Who was Jesus Christ? Why did he come?*

**A** The Christian church as answered this question many times in the last 2,000 years. The church's answer has taken the form of many creeds or confessions of faith. The most well-known of the creeds, the Apostles' Creed, says:

"I believe in Jesus Christ, His only Son, our Lord, who was conceived by the Holy Ghost, born of the Virgin Mary, suffered under Pontius Pilate, was crucified, dead and buried; He descended into Hell; the third day He rose again from the dead; He ascended into heaven, and sitteth on the right hand of God the Father Almighty; from thence He shall come to judge the quick and the dead."

Dr. Martin Luther explained this portion of the Apostles' Creed with these words:

"I believe that Jesus Christ, true God, begotten of the Father from eternity, and also true man, born of the Virgin Mary, is my Lord, who has redeemed me, a lost and condemned creature, purchased and won me from all sins, from death, and from the power of the devil; not with gold or silver, but with His holy, precious blood and with His innocent suffering and death, that I may be His own and live under Him in His Kingdom, and serve Him in everlasting righteousness, innocence, and blessedness, even as He is risen from the dead, lives and reigns to all eternity. This is most certainly true."

To learn more about this God/man and what he can do for you, you should:

Alone—read the Bible. (we suggest the Gospel of St. John first)
With a friend—talk about your Bible reading.
With a group—join a church and work together in the kingdom of God.

# Hey, God, What About Your JUDGMENT?

 **Q** *Does God completely reject a person after his day of judgment if that person has rejected God during his life on earth? If so, does this mean God is not all-loving?*

**A** Another way of putting your questions would be: "Does God give a second chance to the sinner after the Day of Judgment? The answer of the Bible is a clear "NO." For "it is appointed for men to die once, and after that comes judgment" (Heb. 9:27).

Does that mean that, because people get what they deserve on the Day of Judgment, God is unloving? After all that God has revealed to us about His eternal love for sinners, this student of the Bible answers this question with a clear "NO." God so loved the world that He gave it His *only* Son. God did not send His only Son into the world to condemn the world. He sent His only Son to save the world, so that we sinners might have eternal life in Him. Look at John 3:16-18.

The judgment that will befall those who are not "in Christ" is for refusing the forgiveness and the life that God offers in Christ. It is not for denying the existence of God. Those who refuse what God freely offers them will have to "go it alone." About such "going it alone" Jesus said: "How often would I have gathered your children together as a hen gathers her brood under her wings, and *you would not*" (Matt. 23:37). In Acts 13:46 St. Paul tells us that those who cast God's Word aside are those who *judge themselves* unworthy of eternal life.

Do not think that God is pleased that so many people die eternally in their sins. Remember that people are not puppets of God. Remember also that besides being love, God is also holy. His love does not compromise His holiness. Don't test His holiness, Accept His love, in Christ Jesus.

# Hey, God, What About LONELINESS?

**Q** *I have been a Christian for two years. Last year the Lord brought a Christian girl into my life. She is the only girl I have ever felt strongly about. I almost proposed to her. I like her very much. And she is the first girl to ever return that liking. I realize that God does not want us to have a permanent husband-wife relationship, but He just wants us to have a friend-friend relationship.*

*Now she is leaving. I will probably not see her very much as she lives about an hour away from my house. I feel so lonely and lost without her. She has been so much in my life this past year. How do I know what God has in store for me? How do I cope with this feeling of loneliness and sadness?*

**A** During one's lifetime one experiences many times when a pleasure can no longer be enjoyed. The longer one lives the more such experiences one has. If you have had an experience like you have described, you can have some feeling for the sense of loss that a man or woman feels when he or she loses his/her spouse in death. The loved one is deeply missed and will never be replaced.

In such circumstances one must remember that we can *always* depend upon God. He promised that He will never leave or forsake us. We can always depend upon Him. There is no void so big that He cannot fill it. Jesus is the remedy for all our faults; He has borne all our sorrows and all our griefs.

Today you should be grateful that you were able to enjoy the Christian fellowship of the fine individual you described. Thank God that you had such a friendship, and plan to cultivate friendships with other people, both men and women, based on what you have learned in your association with the special friend who has left. If you are a compassionate, trustworthy, and dependable person you can be sure that you will find others with whom you can develop a strong bond.

In the Bible God reveals that it is His will that all people be saved. He wants His people to serve Him in productive ways here on earth and then live with Him forever in heaven. He does not, however, give details as to what we are to do with our lives, beyond serve Him with gladness according to the guidelines of His commandments. We need to develop the abilities He has given us and use them to God's glory and for the benefit of our fellow men. Jesus urged His followers to be other-directed. He does not want us to be turned in upon ourselves. Hence, develop and use your abilities so that you will be able to give a good accounting of your stewardship when He comes again. Such other-directed development and use of your abilities will help you not to feel lonely.

## Hey, God, What About LOVING Too Much?

 *Is it possible to love a person too much? I don't mean sexually, what I mean in a sense of over-protection.*

 It is indeed possible to be over-protective toward someone you love. Such over-protection prevents the loved person from being unique. It prevents learning and growing and would be patronizing and overbearing.

It is only in our relationship to God as our Father that a patronizing love is absolutely correct. It is absolutely correct because, unlike people, God Himself is perfect and knows exactly what is best for us. Since His love is perfect, He cannot be overbearing toward us. It is in Jesus that we come to know the perfect love of God the Father.

In all things, the Christian is one who strives to do what is pleasing in His heavenly Father's sight. That includes the way in which we show our love toward others. We will love them and respect their individuality whether they are our superiors, our peers, or our subordinates. In humility we will also recognize that since our love is not perfect we will not always insist on our way in our relationship with those we love.

## Hey, God, What About LUTHER'S "Anti-Semitism?"

**Q** *How could Martin Luther, obviously a devout Christian, justify his extreme anti-Semitism?*

**A** Christians, and Lutherans in particular, do not think that every utterance of Martin Luther was inspired by God. Luther himself admitted that he was by no means perfect. The things Luther said or may have said about Jews are not always pleasant in our ears.

However, the things Luther said about Jews had mainly to do with their opposition to the Gospel and their rejection of Jesus as their Messiah. In some places Luther refers to Jews and Muslim together. We in the 20th century realize that Jews and Muslim are not bosom buddies. Luther finds fault with them both because they both reject Jesus as Savior. He wrote of them both going to hell because they did not accept the one and only way of salvation that is in Christ Jesus. We think this is the proper understanding of what today sounds like anti-Semitic comments in Martin Luther's writings.

However, Luther's justification of himself, and even our justification of him, is not the last word. The last word is God's Word, according to which Martin Luther and every one of us is justified by God's grace for Jesus sake. Neither Luther nor we can ever think that we will be saved (made right with God) because we are good or devout. It is God alone who is good. His mercy endures forever. Martin Luther trusted in the grace of God. Anyone in whom the Holy Spirit has worked saving faith trusts in the grace of God. That grace covers *all* our sins and all our inconsistencies. Praise God for that, for who among us would be saved, if it were not for the grace of God.

## Hey, God, Are You MANUFACTURED?

**Q** *What do you think of the saying that goes "God is man-made?"*

**A** Certainly men have always made gods in their own image. They have hewn them from stone and carved them out of wood. They have manufactured their own gods and have fallen down and worshiped them. They asked their gods to bless and to save them. In Isaiah 44 and elsewhere in the Bible you can read about such man-made gods. Isaiah calls such gods nothing. They are nonentities, and the Bible strictly forbids those who worship the Lord Jehovah to worship such idols.

A step-up from the primitive worship of idols might be the worship of the sun, the moon, the stars, etc. The worshiper of the sun might conclude that he needs the sun for light, for warmth, for food, and for life, etc. and therefore feels it is proper to worship the sun as the source and the sustainer of life. But worshiping the sun is worshiping the creature rather than the Creator, the gift rather than the Giver. Worshiping the sun would be considered foolish by both the materialist and the Christian, because both know that as powerful as the sun is, it is still a creature, just like all the other extraterrestrial bodies in the universe.

You may also know that the Greeks made gods in their own image and that the Greek gods were far from paragons of virtue. They were conceived as being stronger than men but they had most of the human failings.

The spiritual forefather of Lutherans, Dr. Martin Luther, gave us an explanation of the First Commandment which reminds us that when we fear, love, and trust in a thing above all else, that thing has become our god. It is clear that Dr. Luther had in mind the Bible passages which say that men make gods of their own bellies, their own desires, and their own imaginations (Phil. 3:19; Rom. 16:18).

However, do you really think that man could manufacture the God of the Bible?

| When man is: | While God is: |
|---|---|
| 1. not sufficient of himself; | 1. completely self-sufficient; |
| 2. finite; | 2. infinite; |
| 3. at best imperfect and at worst downright depraved; | 3. perfect; |
| 4. blown about by every wind of fad and fashion; | 4. unchanging; |
| 5. weak in the face of the tremendous power of the universe; | 5. all-powerful; |
| 6. unjust; | 6. just; |
| 7. partial and self-centered; | 7. impartial, merciful; |
| 8. has a beginning and will die; | 8. eternal; |
| 9. impatient; | 9. patient; |
| 10. holds grudges. | 10. merciful, gracious. |

The Bible clearly states that no one has seen God at any time (John 1:18; 1 John 4:12), but it also tells us that Jesus Christ makes the unseen, unseeable God known to us. Jesus is the only One who makes the incomprehensible God known to us humans. One who knows God in Jesus Christ cannot claim that he fully understands God. Neither can he claim that he can fully explain God's nature to another finite human being. The Christian, rather, is one who simply knows that God is love, and that God has been good to him. The Christian is one who is very happy to share with anyone who is interested what the Bible tells us about the nature of God.

## Hey, God, What About MASTURBATION?

**Q** *What does the Lord say about self-masturbation? Does it incur sin?*

**A** Since the Bible is our only sure source of knowing what the Lord God thinks on a certain subject, and since the Bible does not even use the word masturbation, it is difficult to give an absolute statement on this issue. Our modern English word masturbation comes from the Latin *masturbastio* and *masturbatus*. In *Webster's New World Dictionary*, page 905, masturbation is defined as: "Genital self-excitation, usually by manipulation; autoerotism: also called self-abuse, onanism."

Since there is no direct reference to masturbation in the Bible, it is necessary to make a God-pleasing decision on this matter from what is implied in the Bible. The first two chapters of the Bible imply that masturbation is not according to God's design for the proper use of sex.

In Genesis 1 we read that when God created mankind in His own image He created *them*. He created man as male and female (Gen. 1:27). The "image of God" concept can be said to include the idea that neither male nor female are complete in themselves. In Genesis 2 we read that even in his perfect pre-fall state the Lord God said of Adam: "It is not good that the man should be alone; I will make him a helper fit for him" (Gen. 2:18). God wanted man to have a companion. He did not want him to be alone. Thus, for completion, it is natural that a man and a woman should be drawn to each other. Though it is possible for a male or a female to arouse themselves sexually, that is not natural and is not what God had in mind. Masturbation can thus be said to be contrary to God's design for the proper use of sex.

In the New Testament masturbation *may* be included in the warnings about "uncleanness" found in Romans 1:24 (KJV); Romans 6:19 (KJV); Galatians 5:19 (KJV). In Galatians 5:19 "uncleanness," adultery, fornication, and lasciviousness are referred to as works of the flesh. The works of the flesh are against the fruit of the Spirit and are obviously to be regarded as sins. In Ephesians 5:5 (KJV) we are told that no "whoremonger" or "unclean person" or "covetous man" has any inheritance in the kingdom of God and of Christ. Masturbation may also be included in the things done in secret of which Paul says in Ephesians 5:12 that it is a shame to speak.

The person who searches Holy Scripture cannot say for certain that masturbation is sin, but since it seems to be associated with the abuse of the God-given gift of sex, the Christian would not want to sanction such a self-centered activity. The Christian would rather urge the person who participates in any questionable activity: "Awake, O sleeper, and arise from the dead, and Christ shall give you light" (Eph. 5:14).

## Hey, God, What About the Eternity of MATTER?

**Q** *Law of Conservation of Matter: matter cannot be destroyed. There is matter today. Was there matter before God created the world? Is God matter?*

**A** Your questions are scientific, philosophical, and theological at the same time. The answers offered below are given from a theological base, with some knowledge of scientific and philosophical matters.

According to the Bible there was *nothing* before God created all things. God created all things by calling them into being by His Word, His command, His decree (Gen. 1; Heb. 11:3; 2 Pet. 3:5). Hence, there was no matter before the creation, and God is not matter. God is a spirit.

The Law of Conservation of Matter (and Energy) is observable. It is also called the First Law of Thermodynamics. It is called a law rather than a theory because it can be demonstrated. On the basis of the First Law of Thermodynamics it is not possible to postulate a beginning, much less an evolution of things. The idea that matter is eternal is not new; Greek philosophers held that view centuries ago.

The eternity of matter might be tenable if it were not for the second Law of Thermodynamics, which teaches that there is a tendency toward disorder and randomness in any system. This tendency is called entropy; it is the very opposite of evolution. According to the Second Law of Thermodynamics any system left to itself will become less organized and less useful. So, while the total matter/energy is constant (First Law of Thermodynamics), the usable matter/energy decreases as the matter/energy is used. While matter is not destroyed when you burn oil or wood, it is not as useful after the burning as it was before. We are presently plagued by an energy crises for just this reason.

If you extend the trend of more and more entropy forward one can postulate that our universe will run out of usable energy, and it will die a "heat death." If you extend the trend backward in time, you can postulate that at one time the total matter/energy and the usable matter/energy were the same. Note the diagram that follows.

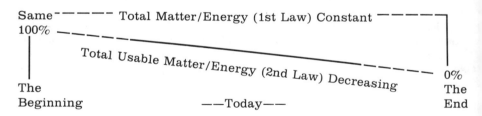

Same ⎯ ⎯ ⎯ ⎯ Total Matter/Energy (1st Law) Constant ⎯ ⎯ ⎯ ⎯ ⎤
100% ⎯ ⎯ ⎯ ⎯ ⎯
   Total Usable Matter/Energy (2nd Law) Decreasing ⎯ ⎯ ⎯ ⎯ 0%
The                  The
Beginning          ⎯⎯Today⎯⎯            End

What this scientific statement suggests to this student of the Bible is that there was a beginning (of all things) and that there will be an end (of all things). The beginning was when God created all things by His almighty Word (Gen. 1:1). The end will come when He withdraws the support of His Word from all things.

I believe that only God is eternal. Yet, I also believe that He freely offers eternity to all people. He offers eternity, or eternal life, to us as a gift in Christ Jesus. Do you know that you need that gift? Have you accepted God's offer of immortality? It is an offer you should not refuse.

# Hey, God, What About Women as MINISTERS?

 *What is the feeling of the church about women ministers?*

Today it depends upon what "church" you are asking about. It is quite obvious that in recent years some church denominations now feel that it is proper for a woman to serve as a minister. However, historically, church denominations including the one of which the authors are members, have felt that it is not appropriate for a woman to serve in the office of the ministry. The conviction of our church, The Lutheran Church—Missouri Synod, is based on its understanding of the following passages of Holy Scripture.

In the very beginning of the Bible "... The Lord God said, 'It is not good that the man should be alone; I will make him a helper fit for him'" (Gen. 2:18).

In 1 Timothy 2:12* we read that women are not to teach or have authority over men in the church. This is because in the family and in the church, which is the family of God, the woman's role is that of helper.

In 1 Timothy 3:2-4** the bishop, or pastor, is to be the husband of one wife and he is to manage his own household well. Later in the same chapter it is stated that the deacon is also to be the husband of one wife and is to manage his own household well. Here we see that both in the family and in the church it is the man who is to be the leader.

In Titus 1:5-9*** the qualifications of those who are to be appointed as elders and bishops are stated. In this section it is again obvious that the spiritual leaders are to be men, not women.

In 1 Corinthians 14:34-35**** it is stated that in the church, men, not women, are to take the leadership role. Husbands are to speak for all members of their families. This section again shows the consistency between the family and the church. Both the family and the church are institutions of God, and there should not be conflict in the role of men and women in each of these institutions. The wife is to be subject to her husband and the husband is to love his wife (Eph. 5:21-33). The husband is compared to Christ, the the wife is compared to the church. In neither the church nor the family should there be two heads.

The reason some people do not like what the Bible has to say on this subject is that they have "bought" the evolutionary notion of "the survival of the fittest."

The Bible does not teach the theory of evolution, the "survival of the fittest," or that men are to be leaders in the family and the church because

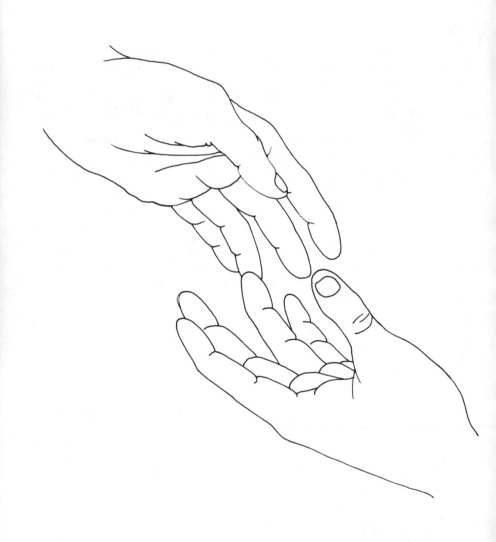

they are stronger or smarter. The Bible does teach that men are to be the leaders in the family and the church because that is God's design for mankind from Genesis 2 until the end of time.

(*1 Tim. 2:12) "I permit no woman to teach or to have authority over men; she is to keep silent."

(**1 Tim. 3:2-4) "Now a bishop must be above reproach, the husband of one wife, . . . He must manage his own household well, . . ."

(***Titus 1:5-6) ". . . and appoint elders in every town as I directed you, if any man is blameless, the husband of one wife, and his children are believers . . . ."

(****1 Cor. 14:33-35) ". . . As in all the churches of the saints, the women should keep silence in the churches. For they are not permitted to speak, but should be subordinate, as even the law says. If there is anything they desire to know, let them ask their husbands at home. . . ."

## Hey, God, What About MIRACLES?

*If Jesus did indeed work miracles, as recorded in the Bible, are there not other accounts of them besides the Scriptures, perhaps by non-Christians? It would prove his deity and power to non-believers if there were historical accounts of his miracles. Are there any? Surely, a man who raises the dead would have some recognition.*

Thank you for this challenging question. This pastor will attempt an answer using the understanding that the Lord has given him.

Jesus performed miracles in order to help people in need. He did not perform miracles for theatrics or in order to impress or "wow" people. As a result it is understandable that those who were not the followers of Jesus would not report His miracles, as they had other "explanations" for what he had done.

Jesus had many opportunities to publicly perform miracles to impress the leaders of the day. He always refused. Jesus refused to perform a miracle for King Herod (Luke 23). There is a particularly good interpretation of this part of Luke 23 in *Jesus Christ Superstar*. Elsewhere we can read that He always refused to perform miracles for the scribes and the Pharisees. One of his last public acts was to refuse to come off the cross when taunted by the crowd.

Jesus also took many opportunities to perform miracles publicly. Read the accounts of the marriage at Cana, the feeding of the 5,000, the healing of the blind man, etc. However, most were done in such an unostentatious manner that nonbelievers were not impressed. We also note that He frequently told the people who benefited from the miracle to do what the Law said to do, but *NOT* to tell how the miracle was performed.

From the above we can see that the purpose of a miracle was to confirm the faith and help the needy, not impress or "wow" the leaders or unbelievers.

It is almost true that not one unbeliever saw the risen Christ. That appears to have been the way He Himself wanted it. Yet, when the apostles began to preach that Jesus, who, as everyone knew, had been crucified, was alive, the first opponents of Christianity did not produce the decaying body of Jesus, as the opponents of Christ and of His followers knew that the grave was empty. The report of the guards being "paid off" by the chief priest in Matthew 28:11-15 indicates that a story had to be made up in order to explain away the empty tomb. This is an example of how those who did not believe in Jesus concocted their own "explanations" of miracles. Despite the "story" about the disciples stealing Jesus body, there is no report of either the soldiers being put to death for sleeping on guard duty, or of any disciple being arrested for grave-robbing. When the apostles preached on the Day of Pentecost, 50 days after Easter, nobody challenged what they said about a risen Christ. Everyone knew that Jesus' body was no longer in Joseph's tomb.

As indicated above, almost no unbelievers saw Jesus after His resurrection. However, Jesus did show Himself to Thomas, who insisted that he would not believe until he saw Jesus. Jesus also appeared to one of the most dedicated opponents of the early church. This man persecuted Christians because he was convinced that they were preaching heresy and blaspheming the only true God. He held that it was contrary to the will of God to call Jesus Lord. However, that great unbeliever, Saul of Tarsus, became Paul, the great missionary and writer of the New Testament. In his letters he tells of his unbelief, his overt opposition to the good news of Jesus, his persecution of Christians and of his dramatic meeting with Christ (Acts 9) which led to a complete turnaround.

## Hey, God, What About MONOGAMY?

**Q** *Is the practice of monogamy (as opposed to polygamy) merely a tradition which we Christians follow, or does the Bible specifically command not to have more than one wife/husband?*

**A** Monogamy (one wife/husband at a time) is God's plan for marriage, according to many passages in the Bible.

It is God's intention that a man leave his father and his mother and cleave unto his wife (Gen. 2:18-25). Thereby he and his wife become one flesh. Notice the singulars; notice also that one and one make one in God's design for marriage.

The New Testament's positive and beautiful statement on marriage is in Ephesians 5:22-33, where the relationship of husband and wife is compared to that of Christ and the church. In verse 31 it is stated that the two shall become one flesh.

From both the Old and the New Testament we can see a clear and consistent statement that one man and one woman are a family. Therefore, it is God's plan that Christians practice monogamy!

## Hey, God, What About MURDER Victims?

**Q** *What does God do to innocent people who are murdered? (With all of the killing in recent years I am just curious.)*

 **A** Revelation 14:13: "Blessed are the dead who die in the Lord."

On the basis of this passage and many others in the Word of God I am convinced that those who die trusting in Jesus as Savior (that's "in the Lord") are blessed. Nothing, not even death can separate us from the love of God which is in Christ Jesus.

That said, I do not think that being a follower of Jesus exempts me from the possibility of being murdered. Only God knows how many of His people have been tortured, slaughtered, raped, and otherwise abused. God "never promised us a rose garden." In fact, Jesus has told His followers that they can expect to be persecuted just because they follow Him. If one follows Jesus, one can expect troubles that one who does not follow Jesus will not experience. Hence, I do not think that the terrible act of being murdered could not happen to you or me.

What does God do with one whose life has been unjustly taken? That depends upon the murdered person's personal relationship to Jesus Christ. It is the same whether the person is murdered, killed in an accident, or dies from natural causes. If that person during life has accepted Jesus Christ as the payment for his/her sins, that individual is saved (safe). If, however, that person has not accepted Jesus Christ, then that person will receive the just reward for his/her sins. The only way to be blessed in death is to be with and in the Lord Jesus at death.

Do you know Jesus as your personal Savior and key to heaven?

# Hey, God, What's Your NAME?

 **Q** *In the Old Testament, why in some parts is God referred to as Jehovah and not in others?*

**A** The two most common ways of referring to God in the Old Testament are "God" and "the Lord." The original Hebrew words are *elohim* and *adonai*, respectively. In many places the two words appear together and are usually translated "the Lord God." However, neither of these words is used exclusively for the only true God. Both *elohim* and *adonai* are used for false gods and men.

Jehovah, Yahweh, or YHWH is God's name. Moses asked: "If I come to the people of Israel and say to them, 'The God of your fathers has sent me to you,' and they ask me 'What is His name?' what shall I say to them?" God answered: "I am who I am." "And He said, 'Say this to the people of Israel, 'I am has sent me to you.'" (Ex. 3:13-14).

In the original Hebrew, which does not have characters for vowels, the "I AM" is four letters, YHWH. "I AM" or "I AM THAT I AM" is the translation of the Divine Name. In the King James Version of the Old Testament you will occasionally find "the LORD" in all capital letters. That is an indication that YHWH is in the original Hebrew.

This practice of substituting "LORD" for Yahweh in the King James Version and other versions reflects the Old Testament practice of rarely speaking God's name. It was not even read when it appeared in the text of the Bible. The reason that God's name was not spoken was that the people did not want to take the chance of breaking the Commandment which reads "You shall not take the name of the Lord your God in vain" (Ex. 20:7). People in Old Testament times figured that if you never spoke the divine name, then you could never be found guilty of taking it in vain. Jewish people have always had the highest regard for the name of God.

C. K. Barrett, in *The New Testament Background*, page 161, indicates that the only day on which the divine name was spoken with the proper vowels was on the Day of Atonement, or Yom Kippur.

Therefore, Jehovah is not very common in the Old Testament because it was held in the highest regard by the Jewish people. Most of the other ways of referring to God in the Old Testament are titles, and their use was not considered a possible breaking of the commandment.

## Hey, God, What About an OBSESSION?

 *I am the same person who wrote the question about loneliness. I have this obsession that it is not a narcotic, but is just as strong and sometimes stronger.*

*I have created this illusion where I take superman and do everything imaginable to him, physically, mentally, sexually. I get a good deal of sexual and physical happiness from it.*

*I realize that it is sin. But when I am doing something I don't really want to do (like study) or when I feel insecure, this illusion really seems appealing.*

*I have used Jesus' power of blood over this temptation. But how can I rid myself of this sin completely (not just temporarily)?*

If you read your own question as another person reads it, you would see that your question shows an obsession with sex. Obsession with any one aspect of life, such as with eating, drinking, even working, leads to an unbalanced life, in which the obsession becomes your god. Obsessions then are sins against the First Commandment: "You shall have no other gods before me" (Ex. 20:3).

If your experience with the girl you described in the other question was as worthwhile as you said it was, then what you learned from your association with her should help you deal with the war that seems to be going on inside of you. If you had a good relationship with someone of the opposite sex, then you realize that sex is not the "be all and end all" that so many people make it today. What you refer to is lust, and lust is the very opposite of love.

"Love is patient and kind; love is not jealous or boastful; it is not arrogant or rude. Love does not insist on its own way; it is not irritable or resentful; it does not rejoice at wrong, but rejoices in the right. Love bears all things, believes all things, hopes all things, endures all things" (1 Cor. 13:4-7).

To paraphrase this we could say that lust is impatient and unkind; lust is jealous and boastful; it is arrogant and rude. Lust insists on it own way; it is irritable and resentful; it rejoices at wrong but hates right. Lust bears nothing, believes nothing, hopes nothing, endures nothing.

We would advise you to become involved in many different ways with members of the opposite sex, so that you will learn to respect, appreciate, and depend on them in ways which will help you realize that they are individuals, and not mere objects. Remember, real happiness is not found in using anybody.

It is only in Christ that complete happiness is to be found. When you are in Christ, sin no longer has dominion over you. Sink the roots of your being deeper and deeper into His Word and you will find yourself growing in His grace. Depend on the leading of the Holy Spirit, and you will find that you will be ready to run from sin. You will not want to think of sinful things, much less give the outward appearance of evil.

If you have fallen into sin, don't blame Jesus; His mercy endures forever. He will pick you up. Don't depend upon yourself; depend upon Christ. Every Christian knows that he is not sufficient of himself, but that his sufficiency is of God.


## Hey, God, What About OVERPOPULATION?

**Q** *One Commandment is "Thou shalt not kill," a widely used adage in the fight against abortion. What does the Bibe tell us to do about the millions killed each year because of starvation. Obviously, we cannot by any stretch of the imagination, feed them. Perhaps we should make a passage read "Quit multiplying and learn about the earth."*

**A** The initial quotation is from Exodus 20:13 (KJV), which is known as the Fifth Commandment. This passage is properly applied to the taking of the life of a prebirth human being. Taking this life (a male or female from the moment of conception) for the convenience of another person is weak ethics and morality.

If you regard the Bible as the Word of God, you are not likely to think it is your prerogative to change anything that the Lord has said through the Bible. So, please understand that the Biblical Christian would not want to make Genesis 1:28 say anything but "God blessed them, and God said to them, 'Be fruitful and multiply, and fill the earth and subdue it; . . .'" Viewing the population and hunger problems, some people ask if this commission of God to fill the earth and subdue it has not been fulfilled. It could hardly ever be completely fulfilled, for if we would all stop having children the earth would be emptied of humans in one generation.

Several news items lead us to wonder about the popular "truth" of the relationship between population growth and mass starvation.

For instance, from time to time we read how the Soviet government gives awards to mothers who have raised more than the average number of children. If an atheistic government thinks that it still needs more people to fill and subdue its part of the earth, what then should the Christian response to God's clear statement in Genesis 1:28 be?

In 1970 the U. N. food and agricultural organization reported that the world's farmers could grow enough food to feed 157 billion people. The world's population is only about 4 billion. This tremendous food production potential is a result of the God-given Green Revolution that began in 1968. The obvious problem then is not one of food production, but food distribution. Just as God has given us the way to grow food so also will He give us the way to distribute the food. As our brother's keeper (Gen. 4:9) let us stretch our imaginations and let us pray for and work toward the goal of distributing to the world the abundance that God has given us.

## Hey, God, What About POT (I)?

 *Do you think God really looks down on people who smoke pot for recreational purposes only?*

**A** If you are asking if God is displeased with, does He warn against, and does He condemn as sin the use of marihuana, then this pastor's answer to your question is "yes." That answer is based on what the Bible tells us in Galatians 5, where we read of the perpetual war within us.

In connection with the contrast between the Spirit (God) and the flesh (natural man) we also note the contrast between the fruit of the Spirit and the works of the flesh. In Galatians 5:19-21 there is a long list of "the works of the flesh": "fornication, impurity, licentiousness, idolatry, sorcery, enmity, strife, jealousy, anger, selfishness, dissension, party spirit, envy, drunkenness, carousing, and the like."

The word *pharmakeia* is translated "sorcery" or "witchcraft" (KJV). Our modern English word "pharmacy" is derived from it. Souter's *Pocket Lexicon to the Greek New Testament* defines *pharmakeia* as follows:

"The practice of drugging, drugging; hence, especially, from the use of mysterious liquids, *sorcery, witchcraft,* inextricably combined with idolatry" (p. 273).

In Galatians 5:20 "idolatry" and "sorcery" are mentioned back to back. Playing around (that's what recreational use would be with "pot" or drugs) is dangerous because it is so closely associated with idolatry.

Some people claim that the use of "pot" and other mind-affecting drugs gives them pleasure, peace, joy, relaxation, etc. According to the Bible, the person who has the Spirit does not need such drug-induced "highs." Rather:

"The fruit of the Spirit is love, joy, peace, patience, kindness, goodness, faithfulness, gentleness, self-control; against such there is no law" (Gal. 5:22-23).

All of us want such good things in our lives. The only true way to experience such fruit of the Spirit is to belong to Jesus Christ.

Do you belong to Jesus? Do you know Him as your personal Lord and Savior? Do you have the Holy Spirit?

## Hey, God, What About "POT" (II)?

**Q** *Come on, Jimmy, do you really think marihuana users are sorcerers? If you do, I feel sorry for you.*
*I feel your answer did a lot more harm than good. It placed a lot of guilt on people's understanding of it. Wake up, Jimmy.*

**A** You must understand that in the last question about the recreational use of "pot" this pastor was relating Galatians 5:19-20 to the contemporary use of mind-affecting drugs.

The recreational user of "pot" may not be a sorcerer, but whether he realizes it or not he is fooling around with a kind of sorcery. This pastor, who has a mind that is captive to the Word of God (Luther's expression) sincerely believes that the use of mind-affecting drugs is playing with sorcery (*pharmakeia*) and, therefore, is to be condemned as a work of the flesh. The works of the flesh are contrary to the fruit of the Spirit.

Understand that guilt according to the Bible is not merely a feeling. There is such a thing as real moral guilt which condemns a person to hell. We can be guilty before God even if we do not feel guilty. The only way to resolve a real moral guilt is by the real forgiveness offered to us by God in Christ Jesus. God's real forgiveness belongs only to those who belong to Jesus. Do you belong to Him?

It is your prerogative to disagree with any answer given in this book. The human answerers do not claim personal infallibility. However, if you choose to disagree with valid conclusions drawn from the Word of God, you are taking issue with God. Bible believing Christians are those whose minds are captive to the Word of God. Those who are in Christ pray, "Speak, Lord, for Thy servant hears" (1 Sam. 3:9).

## Hey, God, Must I Go to Church to PRAY?

**Q** *Why must one go to church to pray to God? Can't one skip church and follow God's teachings in the privacy of his own home?*

**A** It is certainly not necessary to go to a church in order to pray. In fact, one is not spiritually healthy if he prays only in a church service or when he is in a church building. If you compare praying to spiritual breathing, you can figure how healthy your spirit is going to be if you "breathe" only one hour a week.

The spiritually healthy person prays often. He remembers the apostle Paul's directive to "pray constantly" (1 Thess. 5:17), and with the psalmist the spiritually healthy person delights in God's Word at all times, not just when he is in church.

You should also know that the purpose of a church service is not to make "brownie" points with God. As Christians we gather together to encourage "one another, and all the more as you see the Day drawing near" (Heb. 10:25). Christians gather to worship God, to share the blessing God has bestowed on them, and to encourage one another to walk by faith and not by sight. Following Jesus is walking by faith. Following Jesus is not always easy, so we need all the spiritual help we can get.

In addition, when one has the conviction that Jesus Christ is Lord, he does not want to hide that conviction (or as you wrote "in the privacy of his own home"). Faith in Jesus is not something to be ashamed of, because if you've got it, you want to share it. The question then is, "Do you trust in Jesus?" If so, you will pray in private and in public worship services. (See also the question on my SUNDAY Obligation.)

## Hey, God, What About My PRAYERS?

**Q** *How can I know God has answered my prayers (besides just faith)? Can He tell me, or show me?*

 **A** The attitude with which we approach God in prayer is very important. We cannot approach God as if we have a *right* to be heard. We must always remind ourselves that Jesus has given us the privilege of approaching God in prayer. That is why we always pray in Jesus' name. It is only in Jesus' saving name that we can submit ourselves and our requests to God. We can demand nothing of God, only request.

With that in mind it is dangerous to pray only when we want something, or when we have figured out exactly what we want. Such demands are not petitions, supplications, or intercessions, as proper prayers should be. When we pray to God we must do so with the attitude that we are prepared to accept what He gives because we know He knows what is best for us. With such an attitude we should be prepared to accept a "NO" answer, as well as a "LATER, NOT AT THIS TIME" answer. Even when God does give us a "YES" answer it may not have been exactly what we had in mind. When we submit ourselves to God in prayer, we must be ready to accept any of the above answers as well as others.

How do we know when or if God has answered the prayers that we have submitted to Him in all humility? The answer of a person who claims that the Bible is the only rule for faith and life and who does not seek new revelations is that he looks to the Word of God for answers from God. It is in the Bible that we can find the assurance that our sins are forgiven and that we have eternal life. One who prays learns from the Bible that God has provided all that we need for our faith and life in Christ. One who prays should be aware that in physical matters too all good gifts are from above and that they come down from the Father of lights (James 1:17). Regardless of how a good gift comes, ultimately it is *of* God. When the Christian who has been praying for a special good thing says, "If it is Your will, O Lord," he can be certain that when he receives it, it is of God. It is then that he understands the depth and the meaning of the common doxology, "Praise God, from whom *all blessings flow*." And he will then continue wholeheartedly: "Praise him, all creatures here below; Praise him above, ye heavenly host: Praise Father, Son, and Holy Ghost" (*The Lutheran Hymnal*, 644).

## Hey, God, What About PREDESTINATION?

**Q** *Clearly, men are given a free choice to receive Jesus and His gift of salvation into their lives. So how come St. Paul keeps talking about "those who are called" and predestination (Romans)?*

**A** Before dealing with the Romans passage, it must be stated that it is not quite so clear that man is *free* to choose Jesus. People are by nature not free; we are enslaved in sin. Before Christ makes us alive we are "dead through . . . trespasses and sins" (Eph. 2:1). And "we were by nature children of wrath, like the rest of mankind" (Eph. 2:3). That is why we can only be saved by grace, as Ephesians 2:8 puts it.

In the fall, man lost his free will, for it was then that sin and death spread to all men (see Rom. 5:12). As a result of the fall the things of God are foolishness to the natural man; in fact, the natural man cannot know the things of God because to know them requires the spiritual discernment that he does not have (see 1 Cor. 2:14). Hence, left to himself, man is utterly lost.

But thank and praise God that He did not leave us to ourselves. He gave us His only Son (John 3:16). He and His salvation are indeed absolutely free gifts. This is clear. And what we could not see, hear, or conceive of, namely "what God has prepared for those who love Him" (1 Cor. 2:9) God has *revealed* to us by His Spirit (1 Cor. 2:10-12). That same Spirit is the one who moves us to confess Jesus as Lord of our lives (1 Cor. 12:3). All of which is God's doing *for* us and *in* us. Hence, we give Him *all* praise and glory for our redemption.

Now to the Romans passage. Romans 8:28-29 is alluded to in the question, and the questioner is not sure how the reference to predestination fits together with the Biblical teaching that salvation is the free gift of God in Christ Jesus. Romans 8:29 fits together with that doctrine very well because both emphasize that our salvation is solely the work of God. Romans 8:29 is not the only place where God choosing those who are saved is mentioned. Note the following:

—Those who know Jesus as Savior have been chosen "before the foundation of the world" (Eph. 1:4).

—Our holy calling was given us "in Christ Jesus before the world began" (2 Tim. 1:9 KJV).

—"God chose you from the beginning" (2 Thess. 2:13).

—"As many as were ordained to eternal life believed" (Acts 13:48).

All of these passages deal with what is called Election, or Election of Grace. Election deals with the teaching that from God's perspective man is saved solely by the grace of God in Christ. While some people assume that if there is an Election of Grace, there must of necessity be an election of or to damnation, such an assumption cannot be based on the teachings of the Holy Scripture. The Scriptures tell us that God would have all men be saved (1 Tim. 2:4) and that He takes no pleasure in the death of a sinner (Ezek. 18:23). Jesus wants all people to come to Him and be saved. When a person is saved it is solely and wholely by the grace of God; however, when a person is lost it is solely and wholely his own fault for rejecting the grace of God in Christ.

The Bible passages that speak of the Election of Grace of those who are saved are understood to have been written for our comfort and security especially in times of affliction and doubt. You who are in Christ Jesus should read them that way. (See also the question of FAITH)

## Hey, God, What About PREMARITAL Sex (I)?

**Q** *Is premarital sex a sin? If so, what type of sin?*

**A** The Bible answers this question very clearly. The answer is that premarital sex is sin against the commandment "You shall not commit adultery" (Ex. 20:14).

Do not think that adultery is something that only someone who is married can commit. Throughout the Old Testament and the New Testament this commandment is applied to abuse of sex by anyone. When Joseph was propositioned by his boss' wife he replied: "How . . . can I do this great wickedness, and sin against God?" (Gen. 39:9).

Joseph was not married at the time, yet he understood that if he gave in to Potiphar's wife's seduction, he would have sinned against her, against her husband, against himself, and against God. He would have sinned against God, because God, the creator of sex, designed it to be used within the bonds of holy matrimony. Any other use of sex is an abuse in the sight of God. It may also be said that had Joseph agreed to commit adultery with Potiphar's wife, he would also have sinned against his wife-to-be.

In the Sermon on the Mount, Jesus made it quite clear that both married and unmarried people can sin against the Sixth Commandment:
"You have heard that it was said, 'You shall not commit adultery.' But I say to you that everyone who looks at a woman lustfully has already committed adultery with her in his heart" (Matt. 5:27-28).

God considers adulterers and fornicators to be in the same "bed": "Marriage is honorable in all, and the bed undefiled; but whoremongers (fornicators) and adulterers God will judge" (Heb. 13:4 KJV).

God will judge each guilty of sin.

If you are guilty of the sin of fornication, be of good cheer, for there is forgiveness with the Lord. As serious as sexual sin is, the abuse of sex is not unforgiveable. Jesus came to save sinners, and many of His first followers were public sinners. The great apostle Paul even calls himself the chief of sinners. In all cases, when they were sorry for their sins, and asked for forgiveness, Jesus forgave them and received them to Himself. He then sent them back into the world with the admonition that they were to sin no more. Are you sorry for your sins?


## Hey, God, What About PREMARITAL Sex (II)?

**Q**

*What exactly is the Lord's feeling towards premarital sex?*


**A**

Sex is a gift of God that is to be used within the bonds of holy matrimony. Premarital sex or extramarital sex is an abuse of that gift. (See also the question on PREMARITAL Sex [I].)

That answer, as well as this answer, is based on teachings of the Bible, in which the Lord God reveals His "feelings" about many subjects. On any subject on which the Bible speaks, the Christian responds with the words of Samuel, "Speak, Lord, for thy servant hears" (1 Sam. 3:9). The Bible has a great deal to say on the subject of sex, both its use and abuse.

Much of what God tells us in His Word on sexual matters does not jive with the playboy-type, permissive thinking of many in our day. Hence, one must make a choice as to which thinking he will follow, that of the world, or that of Jesus.

"I appeal to you therefore, brethren, by the mercies of God, to present your bodies as a living sacrifice, holy and acceptable to God, which is your spiritual worship. Do not be conformed to this world but be transformed by the renewal of your mind" (Rom. 12:1-2).

We pray that the Holy Spirit will guide you to choose the one way—Jesus.


## Hey, God, Are You REAL?

 *Is there really a God?*

It is logical for the ordinary man to ask such a question, for even the apostle whom Jesus loved admits, "No man hath seen God" (John 1:18 KJV).

Does this mean that there either is no God, or that there is no way of knowing Him? The same apostle does not think so because without deep philosophical debate or question he simply states that, "the only Son, who is in the bosom of the Father, He has made Him [God] known" (John 1:18).

Thus, the way Christians answer questions about God is to tell the inquirer about Jesus, because in Jesus people find the One who is "the Way, and the Truth, and the Life" (John 14:6). In Jesus people find the God they want to share with others.

If you do not know Jesus, you do not know God. Jesus and God are revealed to us in the Word of God, the Bible. So to personally know if there is really a God, you will have to read and study the Bible. (We suggest the Gospel of St. John first.) May God the Father send the Holy Spirit to you to lead you to Jesus.

## Hey, God, What About SALVATION Before Christ?

*How do you think people in the Old Testament times were saved—by grace or by the Law?*

*I thought that perhaps they were saved by faith in God, as we are today by believing in Jesus. However, Scripture of the Old Testament sometimes indicates that they were saved by keeping the Law and walking in God's ordinances.*

*What is your opinion?*

Yes, it appears at times that salvation in the Old Testament is by works and not by grace; however, it is my conviction, based on statements like those made by Paul in Romans 4 that salvation has always been by God's grace. "What does the Scripture say? 'Abraham believed God, and it was reckoned to him as righteousness'" (Rom. 4:3).

It was Abraham's trust in God, not his own works, that made him righteous before God.

Romans 4 also indicates that circumcision and the keeping of the Law came after Abraham trusted in God and the blessings He promised. That is the way it was for Old Testament believers. The sequence was 1) trust in the Lord, 2) follow His ordinances, and 3) look forward to the blessings He has promised. That is the way it is still.

The Ten Commandments are in Exodus 20:3-17. Notice, however, what is stated immediately before the Commandments. Exodus 20:2 is pure Gospel, for it tells what God had done for His people. He delivered His people from the house of bondage just as He delivers us from the bondage of sin through Christ Jesus.

I am convinced that from Adam through Abraham, from Moses through Mary, Joseph, Simeon, and Anna (Luke 2:25-38) Old Testament believers were saved by God through their trust (forward looking) in Him who was to come and who did come.

## Hey, God, Is My SALVATION Sure?

*How can I be sure that I am saved?*

To be sure that you are saved you must read God's Good News Book, the Bible. There God promises His disciples (and as a Christian

you are one of His disciples): "Lo, I am with you always, to the close of the age" (Matt. 28:20).

"Neither death, nor life, nor angels, nor principalities, nor things present, nor things to come, nor powers, nor height, nor depth, nor anything else in all creation, will be able to separate us from the love of God in Christ Jesus our Lord" (Rom. 8:38-39).

With these promises, one who accepts Jesus as his Savior and Lord can be certain that God will not forsake him while he lives. Also, in death, we can accept the words of Jesus to the penitent thief on the cross as applying to us: "Truly, I say to you, today you will be with Me in Paradise" (Luke 23:43).

## Hey, God, What About the SECOND [Final] Coming?

 *What will happen at Christ's second [final] coming?*

 A whole lot of things!

The Bible tells us in many ways of the awesome events that are connected with Christ's final coming. So many things are said that it is not always easy to know how it all fits together. For reference sake, the final coming of Christ fits into the the broader category of eschatology, which means "the study of the last things." In fact, we are told so much about the last things in the Bible that this author likes to think of eschatology as a diamond with many facets. As with a diamond, when one looks at it from a different angle one sees something that one may not have seen before, while at the same time one never sees the whole at once.

It seems appropriate to start a consideration of what will happen when Jesus comes again with what Jesus Himself said would happen. In Matthew 24 we read about His final coming and the close of the age. Note the following:

vv. 4-8: speaks of troubles on the earth; Jesus says, however, that this is only the beginning of suffering;
v 9: speaks of the tribulations Jesus' followers will experience;
v. 13: speaks of the end and of those who shall endure until it comes;
v. 14: says that the end will not come until the Gospel is preached throughout the whole world;
vv. 15-26: speaks of more troubles that will happen before the end;
v. 27: in this section Jesus speaks of His coming; He says that it will be as sudden and unpredictable as a flash of lightning;

v. 29: again refers to tribulation and a shake-up of the universe;

v. 30: gives us a sign of the Son of Man; He shall come in the clouds with power and great glory;

v. 31: tells us that angels shall be with Him, that there shall be a trumpet call, that the elect will be gathered from everywhere;

v. 35: speaks of the heaven and the earth passing away;

v. 36: says that only God the Father knows exactly when this will happen;

vv. 37-39: refers to men being as unprepared for the coming of the Son of Man as people were for the coming of the flood;

vv. 40-42: gives a reference to what might be related to the rapture (the Greek *harpazo* of 1 Thess. 4:17, though that Greek word is not used in this text in Matthew);

—what is described here fits together with the gathering of the elect from the four winds in v. 31, and what is given in 1 Thessalonians 4:13-18;

—in v. 42 the hearers are urged to be on the alert at all times because no one knows exactly when the Son of man will come again;

vv. 45-51: tells a brief story about unfaithful servants who are caught unprepared when their master returns home; they are judged and punished.

In Matthew 25 we find two parables, the main point of each being to caution watchfulness for the Lord's coming. In Matthew 25:31-46 Jesus tells what will happen when He comes again in glory. There will be a public separation and judgment of all humans.

In John 6:40 Jesus also speaks of raising up those who believe in Him on the last day; while in Acts 1:9-11 just after His ascension, two messengers, presumed to be angels, tell His disciples that He shall be seen coming again in the same way as He was seen ascending into heaven.

In two of his letters, the apostle Paul deals with Christ's final coming. 1 Thessalonians 4:13-18 says that when Jesus comes again, He will raise up those who died trusting Him, and then He will catch up both them and the believers still alive. They will be caught up in the air to meet the Lord and to be with Him forever. This "catching up" is the rapture. The word rapture is taken from the Greek word *harpazo*. This rapture is connected with Jesus' final coming, not, as some people think, something that takes place before the end.

1 Corinthians 15:51-57 says that at the time of the resurrection not all believers will be asleep (i.e., dead in the Lord). Those who are alive when Jesus comes again will be changed. That change will take place when He catches His own up to meet Him in the air.

2 Peter 3:10 and 12 says that the coming of the day of the Lord is connected with the end or the destruction of the world.

You may have noticed that we have not quoted from the Book of Revelation. That is not because we do not like the Book of Revelation, it is because we feel that the information given us in the Gospels and the

Epistles must be firmly established in our minds before we delve into the mysterious final book of the Bible. The highly figurative language which includes many symbolic numbers must be interpreted in the light of clear Bible passages such as the ones cited above. (See also the question on SIX-Six-Six and the Beast.)

Since Jesus could come at any time, and in fact He even said He would come when least expected (like a thief in the night), the very personal question that each of us must ask ourselves is, "Am I ready?" Are you ready to meet Jesus?

## Hey, God, What About the Fun of SIN?

*In your own words, why are all the "fun" things (sex, pot, gambling, etc.) illegal as far as the Bible goes? Why wouldn't God want us to have a good time? He made us. If He created the fun things to tempt us into damnation, that seems like a pretty cruel thing to do.*

*P. S. I don't mean to sound disrespectful. I'm just a puzzled agnostic.*

Your questions indicate acceptance of two assumptions: one, that the things you list, as well as others you imply, are indeed fun; and two, that pleasure is the highest good.

To begin with I challenge the assumption that the unrestricted and uninhibited use of anything, be it sex, drugs, wine, money, food, etc. is in fact "fun." All these can be properly used, but all can be terribly abused. God in His law has not given us absolute "no-nos" concerning the items you mentioned. For instance, the Sixth Commandment says "You shall not commit adultery" (Ex. 20:14). This does not forbid all use of sex, only adultery and fornication. Some people think that adultery and fornication are "fun," but such thinking ought to be checked against what adultery and fornication do to families, marriages, and individuals. The Sixth Commandment, along with all the other commandments, is intended for our good. Our good does not always coincide with our immediate and often very self-centered compulsion for gratification or "fun" now.

I also challenge the assumption that pleasure is the highest good (hedonism). In our secular, materialistic age people are talking themselves into believing that pleasure is the highest good. It is an article of the "playboy faith" that pleasure is the be-all and end-all. But the works of Alexander Solzhenitsyn tell how long hedonistic people survived and/or what kind of "people" they became when they adopted pleasure as their philosophy of life. Solzhenitsyn holds that truth, right, and human dignity, not pleasure, must be considered among the higher goods, whether in a Soviet prison camp or the United States of America.

Good logic alone guides one to agree that "A is not non-A." Hence, it is logical that if God has in mind for us the good (the fun) of the proper enjoyment of sex (that's A) then He would make known to us that the opposite is bad (that's non-A). That God tells us what the proper use and the improper use of His gifts are, does not seem cruel to this writer. Despite his own personal temptations and sins, the Christian who trusts in Jesus and His Word confesses with the psalmist and the apostle Paul that the law of God is always good.

Lutherans believe that the chief purpose of the law of God is to serve as a mirror. The law of God, which is perfect, shows us our sins like a mirror shows us our dirty face. The Law shows us our sins so that we might see our need for forgiveness and turn to God in repentance. Then the Gospel shows us the grace of God in Christ. God takes no pleasure in the death of a sinner. He would have none be lost. That is why in the "fulness of time" He sent forth His Son to redeem us from the power of sin. Jesus came for all men. Jesus would be your Savior. He would save you so that you can really learn what "fun" is, and have the fullness of joy and pleasures forevermore as He promises those who love Him.

## Hey, God, Are We All SINNERS?

**Q**

*Are we all sinners? Why?*

**A**
It is the all-knowing, holy, and just God who considers all people to be sinners. His standard of judgment is Himself. "You, therefore, must be perfect, as your heavenly Father is perfect" (Matt. 5:48) and "You shall be holy; for I the Lord your God am holy" (Lev. 19:2).

Do you think that any human can measure up to God's standard? Do you think that a human can even measure up to his own standard of perfection? What do you think of the person who thinks he is perfect?

"There is no distinction; since all have sinned and fall short of the glory of God" (Rom. 3:22-23).

Falling short of the glory, the perfection, and the holiness of God is what sin is. Sin is not just our deeds but our words and our thoughts as well.

One of the words for "sin" in the Greek New Testament is an interesting picture-word. That word, *hamartia,* means "missing the mark." We humans sin when we miss the mark with God. We sin when we do not love the Lord God with all our heart, soul, and might, and when we do not love our neighbors as ourselves. We sin when we fail to do the good that we know we ought to do, and we sin when we do those things we know we ought not to do. When we go contrary to God's revealed will, either written on the hearts of all men or written in the Bible, then we feel guilty. We feel guilty because we are guilty.

There is a great deal of talk these days about guilt feelings. There are some people who insist that once you can convince someone that what he has done is not sinful and once we get rid of the word sin, guilt feelings will be erased. Some people have been talking like that for centuries, and still quite a few people feel guilty. They feel guilty despite the fact that intellectually they have convinced themselves that there is no such thing as sin. They *think* they are not guilty, but still they *feel* guilty. Like Lady Macbeth's spot, they cannot get rid of the "damn thing."

Humans cannot get rid of the "damn thing" called guilt, because it is a damn thing. It is a damning thing. Guilt is not merely psychological; it is moral and it is pathological. Guilt haunts us because there is such a thing as sin. We feel guilty because we *are* guilty.

Guilt feelings cannot be just wished away. The only way to resolve guilty feelings, real guilt, and sin is through forgiveness. It is the blood of Jesus Christ that dissolves guilty feelings, real guilt, and sin. In Romans 3, after the Lord comes down hard on us humans for falling short of His glory, He gives the Good News. God always delivers the "bad news" first, then the Good News. The Good News of God in Romans 3:24-26 is that in Jesus there is forgiveness for all our sins. God's forgiveness is free. He gives it to us as a gift. While His forgiveness is free, it is very expensive, because it cost God His only Son.

As real as sin is, even more real is the forgiveness that is to be found in Jesus. That forgiveness is for you. You can enjoy it when you "take Jesus as your Savior." The person who puts his trust in Jesus is the one who does not have to deny the reality of sin and guilt. That person no longer has to use complicated ways of explaining away his own shortcomings. That person does not try to justify his sins. That person admits them, and lays them on Jesus.

All who read this answer are invited to lay their sins on Jesus so that they may receive "the peace of God, which passes all understanding" (Phil. 4:7). (See also the question on my GUILT.)


## Hey, God, What About SIX-Six-Six and the Beast?

**Q** *What does the beast like a lamb in Revelation 13 mean, and what is the significance of 666 in Revelation 13:18\*?*
*\*"This calls for wisdom: let him who has understanding reckon the number of the beast, for it is a human number, its number is six hundred and sixty-six" (Rev. 13:18).*

**A** This answerer must admit that he is not sure what is meant by the beasts and the number 666 in Revelation 13. He is unsure because he accepts the principle of Biblical interpretation that a prophecy is only to be interpreted by its fulfillment. This means that one can only be sure of the meaning of a prophecy in the Bible when the Bible itself gives the fulfillment and tells that it is the fulfillment.

The clearest example of this principle is found in Matthew 1. There the Evangelist tells us that Jesus' birth of the Virgin Mary was in fulfillment of Isaiah 7:14.

As for the beasts and the number 666 in Revelation 13, this pastor finds no clear statement elsewhere in Scripture as to their definite meaning. What is offered below are observations and tentative suggestions as to their meaning.

The beast in the second half of Revelation 13 is introduced in verse 11 as "another beast" to distinguish it from the beast mentioned in verse 1. The first beast arose from the sea, whereas the second one arose from the earth. The second beast was not like a lamb, but he had two horns like a lamb. Eerdman's The New Bible Commentary , page 1185, suggests that the second beast represents the prophets of the first beast, since it causes the inhabitants of the earth to worship the first beast. That makes some sense, but it is difficult to know with whom to identify the second beast.

Revelation 13:18 says that the beast's number is 666. There are probably six hundred and sixty-six explanations of the number 666. Several commentators suggest that the number symbolizes the constant falling short of perfection by the Antichrist and his hosts. Each digit is 1 short of the number 7 which is regarded as the perfect number. The New Bible Commentary suggests that 666 is a symbol of the Hebrew idea of "primal chaos," which seems to be a reference to Genesis 1:2.

At any rate, even without a final interpretation of these passages, one gets a picture of the terrible nature of sin and the terrible consequences of getting caught in the kingdom of darkness. Indeed, even cursory reading of the Book of Revelation should convince the reader that he will not want to get caught under the power of sin. Rather, the reader will want to belong to Christ, who is pictured not as the beast of the world, but as the Lamb of God, and God's conqueror of evil.

That Christ, that Lamb of God, that conqueror of evil is of course Jesus. Do you belong to Him? Do you trust Him? Are you on His side in the struggle against evil in this world?

## Hey, God, What About "a STONE So Heavy?"

 *"How do you answer the question 'Could God make a stone so heavy He couldn't lift it?'"*

 This is an "old saw" that seems like a smart question, but as an "old saw" it is not particularly original.

You and I can roll a snowball so large that we cannot lift it. But if we rolled one that large for the second and third parts of the snowman we would be doing something stupid.

God has revealed in both the creation and in His Word, the Bible, that He is indeed almighty, and as such could make the stone so heavy. However, He has also revealed that He is omniscient (all-knowing and all-wise) and as such He is smart enough not to do such a stupid thing as make such a heavy stone.

God does not do things just to show off. During His earthly ministry, Jesus did many signs and wonders; however, on many occasions He told those who benefited from His miracles not to tell others. When He fed a large crowd one time, He even had to flee because the people were so impressed by what He had done that they wanted to make Him their king. Those people were "wowed" by Jesus' power, but that was not what Jesus had in mind. He wanted them to know that He helped them because He loved them. It was because of God's great eternal love that He sent forth His Son for us. Jesus demonstrated the power of God, but He redeemed us by the love of God. (See also the question on MIRACLES.)

Since Jesus' purpose was to bring men back to God, Christians see all of God's activities through the perspective of His grace toward us. When a person knows that love of God and thinks with the mind of Christ, then the question about the "stone so heavy" is irrelevant.

## Hey, God, What About SUICIDE?

**Q** *Is it true that if you commit suicide, you automatically go to hell because God gave you life and it is not up to you to take it? Then what about those who are soldiers, they may not take their own lives but they deprive others of their life.*

**A** The commandment implied in your questions reads, "You shall not kill" (Ex. 20:13). The Hebrew word for "kill" literally means to take someone's life by spearing or running through in a malicious, deliberate, and premeditated way. Hence, it refers to kill as in murder, and the commandment could read, "You shall not murder."

The commandment is not applied to the accidental taking of life, capital punishment, self-defense, or public defense in a just cause. In Romans 13:1-7 we see that the Lord God considers the government to be his servant and as such it can deliver judgment, including capital punishment, on criminals (sinners). Therefore, a policeman or soldier can, in the defense of his life or in defense of society, take a life and not be acting contrary to the Fifth Commandment.

Your question on suicide is a difficult one to answer, because ordinarily the person who commits suicide does not have a chance to repent of his sin before he dies. Since suicide is self-murder and is thought to be deliberate and premeditated, it is a sin against the Fifth Commandment. However, God alone judges, and since we cannot know the mind of the person in the moment before death, we find comfort in the possibility that forgiveness was requested and received. So it is not automatic that a person who commits suicide will go to hell.

If you have thoughts of suicide, talk to a pastor at once. He can offer you the peace that passes all understanding and that is in Christ Jesus alone. If you do not have a regular pastor, look in the Yellow Pages under Churches and call the nearest church, for God has assured us that when you seek, you will find, when you ask it will be given to you, when you knock (ring) it will be opened to you (Matt. 7:7-8). In the words of the hymn written in 1613 A.D. by Johann Major.

> Alas, my God, my sins are great,
> My conscience doth upbraid me;
> And now I find that in my strait
> No man hath power to aid me.
>
> And fled I hence in my despair
> In some lone spot to hide me,
> My griefs would still be with me there
> And peace still be denied me.
>
> Lord, thee I seek, I merit naught;
> Yet pity and restore me.
> Just God, be not Thy wrath my lot
> Thy Son hath suffered for me.
>
> If pain and woe must follow sin,
> Then be my path still rougher.
> Here spare me not; if heaven I win,
> On earth I gladly suffer.

*The Lutheran Hymnal*, 317:1—4

# Hey, God, What About My SUNDAY Obligation?

 *Can a Catholic go to a Lutheran service on Sunday and fulfill his Sunday obligation?*

To get a Catholic answer to this question you will need to ask a Catholic priest. The answer that follows is a Lutheran answer given by a Lutheran pastor.

First of all, Lutherans do not speak of "obligation" with regard to attendance at services of worship. We speak of *our needs* and of *the blessings* we can enjoy and share with our fellow Christians through public worship services.

What *needs* do we feel we have? We know that this side of heaven we will struggle with sin from within and without ourselves. We get weary in this struggle. We *need* to be strengthened and revived to continue the struggle. We know that in this world we experience troubles, tribulations, and temptations, all of which tear at our trust in God. The world would destroy our faith. Therefore, we know we *need* to be renewed in the grace that initiated our faith (our trust) in Jesus in the first place. At times we feel all alone. We *need* to know that we are not all alone. We *need* the encouragement of our fellows who share the faith. We *need* comfort; we *need* guidance; we *need* forgiveness, we *need* the admonition of the Lord. This list of *needs* is by no means exhaustive; it is intended to be typical.

The *blessings* that God gives us provide for our needs. It is by continuing in the Word of Christ, which is preached at Lutheran worship services, that we continue to be disciples of Christ. God blesses us through His Word, which we share at our worship services. That Word of God comforts, it admonishes, it strengthens, it revives, and it renews. With psalms, hymns, spiritual songs, confession of sin, creeds, and prayers we encourage one another in our lives for Christ. We also enjoy the blessing of Holy Communion in our services. We believe that with the bread and the wine Jesus gives us His true body and blood to assure us of the forgiveness of all our sins and to strengthen our trust in Him. We believe He gives us pardon and peace in the Sacrament of the Altar. All those who have been properly instructed and have prepared themselves are invited to the Supper of our Lord.

If you feel the needs indicated above and would like to enjoy the blessings offered by Lutheran services, you are most cordially invited to join us any Sunday or during Lent and Advent for special midweek services. (See also the question Must I Go To Church To PRAY?)

# Hey, God, What About "TONGUES?"

**Q** *Just exactly what is speaking in tongues?*

**A** "Speaking in tongues" or simply "tongues" is an expression that you'll find in Acts and 1 Corinthians. In the Greek New Testament the word is *glossa*, which simply means "tongue." It usually appears in the plural. The word *glossa* is found 50 times in the New Testament. Half of the time the context indicates that the word is being used in an ordinary sense. In the other half it is obviously being used to refer to something extraordinary.

Alexander Souter in *A Pocket Lexicon to the Greek New Testament*, page 56, gives the following on the word *glossa:*

"(a) *tongue*, especially as an organ of speech;

"(b) *tongue, language;*

"(c) also, usually in the plural, for the unintelligible sounds uttered in spiritual ecstasy."

Souter's third definition seems to be a simple answer to your question.

To arrive at a more thorough answer to what the Bible teaches about "tongues," one must look at the Bible itself. In 1 Corinthians 12:10, 28, 30; 13:8; 14:2, 4-6, 9, 13-14, 19, 22, 26, 39 note the following significant points about "speaking in tongues:"

—it is but one of the variety of gifts and manifestations of the Holy Spirit;

—all believers do not speak in tongues;

—"tongues" will cease;

—speaking in tongues is not addressed to man but to God;

—the "tongues" speaker only edifies himself;

—"tongues" can only be of benefit to others if there is an interpretation;

—"tongues" is not speaking with the mind;

—"tongues" is not a sign for believers but for unbelievers;

—yet at the same time the abuse of "tongues" can cause unbelievers to think that Christians are mad;

—though speaking in tongues is not forbidden, God wants things done decently and in order in His church.

This list of significant points is by no means exhaustive, but is typical.

People of Pentecostal and Neo-Pentecostal persuasion claim that "speaking in tongues" is the indispensable first sign that one has been

baptized in the Holy Spirit. According to their understanding, one cannot be sure that one has received the gift of the Holy Spirit unless one has spoken in tongues.

This teaching of the "second blessing of the Holy Spirit" (after faith in Christ) is regarded by those of us who insist on the objective historical Christian faith as clearly contrary to the apostle Paul's teaching in 1 Corinthians 1:7 that in Christ we have every spiritual gift (Greek *charismata*). The overemphasis on one of the many gifts of the Spirit makes for elitism among the followers of Jesus, an elitism that should not be, because if you have the Son, you have life. If you confess Jesus as your Lord, then you have the Holy Spirit. If you call God your Dad, (*abba* in Mark 14:36 and Rom. 8:15 is Hebrew for father) then the Spirit of God dwells within you. And if you are in Christ, what you need is not to "speak in tongues"; what you need is to let the Spirit of the living God fill and guide every aspect of your life. When you let the Spirit in then you will grow up into your full stature as a man or woman in Christ. (See also the question on CHARISMA)

## Hey, God, What About TRANSCENDENTAL Meditation?

*When Christ said that heaven is within, could he have meant that one can experience heaven through some sort of meditation like transcendental meditation?*

No doubt your connection of transcendental meditation and the Bible statement of heaven within us comes from the passage: "The kingdom of God is within you" (Luke 17:21 KJV).

Your connection is natural. However, a clearer translation of this text is in the Revised Standard Version:

"Being asked by the Pharisees when the kingdom of God was coming, He [Jesus] answered them 'The kingdom of God is not coming with signs to be observed; nor will they say, 'Lo, here it is! or There!' for behold, the kingdom of God is in the midst of you" (Luke 17:20-21).

Preference is given to "the kingdom of God is in the midst of you" because Jesus would hardly have told the Pharisees, who rejected Him, that the kingdom of God (the rule or reign of God) was in them. Preference is also given to this translation because one of the very early versions of the Greek original (the Syriac from the 4th and 5th century A. D.) renders it *"among"* rather than *"within"* you.

Thus, this passage does not teach that heaven is in man. Rather, the Bible as a whole teaches that man is by nature sinful and unclean and that only through the suffering and death of Jesus Christ can we become sinless and clean.

Concerning Transcendental Meditation, it may be said that the Christian is one who rejects any practice which claims to give "God-consciousness" other than that grounded in faith in Jesus Christ. The roots of T. M. are in Hinduism, no matter what the teachers of T. M. say.

T. M. is a religious thing according to Maharishi Mahesh Yogi. In his *Meditations of Maharishi Mahesh Yogi* he writes: "Transcendental meditation is a path to God" (page 59) and "A very good form of prayer is this meditation which leads us to the field of the Creator, to the course of Creation, to the field of God" (page 95).

The initiation ceremony, in which the meditator receives his mantra, is a *form of worship*. Note well the following translation of the Transcendental Meditation's initiation ceremony by David Haddon in "Transcendental Meditation Challenges The Church," *Christianity Today*, March 26, 1976, pp. 15—18.

*"Invocation*

"To LORD NARAYANA, to lotus-born BRAHMA, the Creator . . . to GOVINDA, ruler among the yogis, to his disciple; SHRI SHANKARACHARYA, . . . to the tradition of our MASTERS, I bow down.

". . . To the personified glory of the Lord, to SHANKARA, emancipator of the world, I bow down.

"To SHANKARACHARYA the redeemer, hailed as KRISHNA and BADARAYANA, the commentator of the BRAHMA SUTRAS, I bow down.

"To the glory of the Lord I bow down again and again, at whose door the whole galaxy of gods pray for perfection day and night.

"Adorned with immeasurable glory, preceptor of the whole world, having bowed down to Him we gain fulfillment.

"Skilled in dispelling the cloud of ignorance of the people, the gentle emancipator, BRAHMANANDA SARASVATI, the supreme teacher, full of brilliance, Him I bring to my awareness.

"Offering the invocation to the lotus feet of SHRI GURU DEV, I bow down. . . .

"Offering cloth to the lotus feet of SHRI GURU DEV, I bow down. . . .

"Offering a flower to the lotus feet of SHRI GURU DEV, I bow down. . .

"Offering incense to the lotus feet of SHRI GURU DEV, I bow down. . . .

"Offering fruit to the lotus feet of SHRI GURU DEV, I bow down. . . ."

*"Offering camphor light*

"White as camphor, kindness incarnate, the essence of creation garlanded with BRAHMAN, ever dwelling in the lotus of my heart, the creative impulse of cosmic life, to That, in the form of GURU DEV, I bow down. . . .

"*Offering a handful of flowers*

"GURU in the glory of BRAHMA, GURU in the glory of VISHNU, GURU in the glory of the great LORD SHIVA, GURU in the glory of personified transcendental fulness of BRAHMAN, to Him, to SHRI GURU DEV, adorned with glory, I bow down.

"This translated excerpt of the hymn chanted in Sanscrit by the teacher during the initiation into Transcendental Meditation identifies the initiation as a traditional Hindu 'puja' or worship ceremony. It is also apparent from this text that the particular Hindu tradition followed is that of Shankara, the ninth-century Hindu philsopher-reformer. . . ."

The candidate for initiation brings an *offering* of flowers, fruit, and a clean white handkerchief. In a candle-lit room permeated with incense, he *kneels* before a picture of Guru Dev, Maharishi's dead master. The initiator *kneels* and presents the offering with a *song of thanksgiving* (see above) which honors the departed masters of the Shankara tradition of Hinduism.

Hinduism is panthoistic. Everything, even evil, is a manifestation of the One or the Absolute according to Hinduism. It denies the personal nature of God. Obviously it does not acknowledge Jesus Christ as *the* only way to the Father. Maharishi states in his commentary on the *Bhagavad-Gita*,

"The Lord (Krishna) names faith as a prerequisite to knowledge" (page 316) and ". . . the Lord (Krishna) declares that realization of the state of all knowledge is the only way to salvation—there is no other way" (page 228) to ". . . bring faith to the faith*less*" (page 319).

As a Christian you are full of faith in Jesus. If you accept and practice Transcendental Meditation, you will contradict your faith in Christ.


## Hey, God, What About Your TRIUNE Nature?

 *I tend to recall that in Genesis concerning the creation of man the words "we shall make him in our image" is stated. Who does "we" and "our" refer to?*

What you have recalled is Genesis 1:26-27, which reads: "Then God said, 'Let *Us* make man in *Our* image, after *Our* likeness; and let them have dominion over the fish of the sea, and over the birds of the air, and over the cattle, and over all the earth, and over

every creeping thing that creeps upon the earth.' So God created man in His own image, in the image of God He created him; male and female He created them."

The plurals found in verse 26 have raised questions in the minds of many people for a long time. Who was God speaking to? Was there anyone else with whom He could converse? Was he talking to the angels?

From the perspective of the New Testament, Christians understand the plurals in Genesis 1:26 to be a very early unexplained reference to the mystery that God's nature is triune. Hence, we think that when God was contemplating creating man, the Father, the Son, and the Holy Spirit discussed the matter. Thus, we say that God was talking to Himself in Genesis 1:26.

Such a thing does not sound strange when you remember that in the New Testament we learn that Jesus was involved in the creation of all things (John 1:1-3; Col. 1:15-17). That is why in one of its creeds the Christian church confesses that Jesus is "God of God, Light of Light, Very God of Very God."

The Holy Spirit was also involved in the creation. In Genesis 1:3 we are told that the Spirit of God moved over the face of the waters. So, in the Nicene Creed, Christians have confessed that the Holy Spirit is "the Lord and Giver of Life."

The Hebrew word for God is *elohim* in the Old Testament, and that word is itself a plural. Even in the basic Old Testament confession of faith, the *Shema* (Hebrew for "hear"), we read: "Hear, O Israel: The Lord our God is one Lord" (Deut. 6:4).

The emphasis on the oneness of God stresses the concept that God is a unity. Jesus never went against basic Old Testament teaching. Neither did He go against the Old Testament when He commissioned His followers to make disciples by baptizing "in the *name* of the Father and of the Son and of the Holy Spirit" (Matt. 28:19). Note that "name" is singular, yet He gives three names. Jesus did not see His commission as contrary to the Old Testament; rather, He saw His teachings as the fulfillment of the Old Testament.

The interrelationship of the Old and New Testaments is referred to in an interesting way by an early convert to Christ. St. Augustine of Hippo said that the New Testament is concealed in the Old Testament, while the Old Testament is revealed in the New Testament (*The Reply to Faustus, the Manichaean*, XXII, 76—77).

## Hey, God, What About TROUBLED Times?

 *How can I tell if God is helping me in troubled times?*

 God invites us to speak to Him in times of trouble and has promised to hear and answer.

"Call upon Me in the day of trouble; I will deliver you, and you shall glorify Me" (Ps. 50:15).

"Ask, and it shall be given you; seek, and ye shall find; knock, and it shall be opened unto you" (Matt. 7:7 KJV).

"The Lord is nigh unto all them that call upon him, to all that call upon Him in truth. He will fulfill the desire of them that fear Him; He also will hear their cry, and will save them" (Ps. 145:18-19 KJV). (See also the question on PRAYERS).

## Hey, God, What About UZ and Buz?

*Who were Uz and Buz (mentioned in the Old Testament)? From what family are they, and who were their parents?*

Uz and Buz are mentioned together in Genesis 22:21. They are listed among the eight sons of Milcah and Nahor. Uz is said to be the first born while Buz is said to be Uz's brother.

The context indicates that Nahor, the father of Uz and Buz, was the brother of Abraham. Hence, Uz and Buz were nephews of the first patriarch. Beyond these simple facts we know nothing about them.

Why then, are these rather obscure individuals mentioned in the Bible? Why, because individuals are important to God! When you know that your name appears in a list of names in a newspaper article, you will look for it until you find it, because your name is important to you.

The many lists of names in the Bible demonstrate that God is interested in us as individuals. In fact, Jesus, the Good Shepherd, knows and calls His sheep by name (John 10:3).

Read God's Book and I am sure you will find that God is speaking directly to you. His Law will come down hard on you, but his Gospel will show you that Jesus loves you and does indeed call *you* by name.

## Hey, God, What About Occasional VICE?

*Hello, I wrote the question "Why Are 'Fun' Things SIN?" and with all due respect, it seems that all your answers just fall back on the Bible. It would be nice to hear an answer in plain everyday language for us religious laymen (agnostic too). With all your knowledge of the Bible it seems your opinions would suffice. I would like to hear a plain "unquoted" answer as to why anyone should avoid indulging in vices once in a while.*

Thank you for an apparently unintended compliment. We are pleased that you feel that all our answers to moral and spiritual concerns "fall back on the Bible" because it is the express purpose of this book to faithfully communicate teachings of the Word of God. However, we are saddened that you are not willing to accept what the Word of God teaches as the answer of God to such concerns. It is not intended that this book be a platform for the opinions of the answerers. Rather, it is intended that the questioners be directed to the appropriate words of God to answer their questions.

Your word "vice" is defined as "a moral fault or failing; especially immoral conduct of habits, as in the indulgence of degrading appetites" (*Webster's 1941 Collegiate Dictionary*, page 1117). Further it is: "1) a serious fault of character: grave moral failing; 2) evil or wicked conduct; corruption; depravity; 3) a particular immoral, depraved, or degrading habit" (*Webster's 1968 New World Dictionary of the American Language*, p. 1624). Vice is one of the "either or" situations in life. You either are indulging in vice or you are not. There is no such thing as a little bit of vice, any more than there is such a thing as being a little bit immoral. You either are or you are not. Despite the fact that some people call certain vices "fun," in God's sight a sin is a sin is a sin. Vice, no matter in what form or quantity, is destructive, debilitating, and damning. Since God does not want such dire consequences to befall us, He tells us, for our own good, not to indulge in vice.

But God does much more than tell us what is bad for us and displeasing to Him. He has good news for us. The Good News is that Jesus Christ is the One who can deliver every man and every woman from every sin. In Jesus we can have victory instead of defeat, strength instead of weakness, and life rather than damnation.

You see, only when one is in Christ does he realize that Jesus is stronger than sin. As one grows in Christ, one is less and less attracted to sin. The temptation to sin is never completely overcome in this life for in this life the Christian is one who is always in the process of "becoming." The Christian is not perfect, but he is aware of the direction in which he is moving. The Christian knows that this positive direction is far better, far more meaningful, and far more fulfilling, than the negative direction in which those who indulge in vice are going. Friend, do not choose vice and the road that leads to damnation. Choose Jesus, for He is *the* Way to eternal life.

## Hey, God, What About My VOCATION?

*How can one know what is God's will for an individual's vocation in life? I know if I work hard at studying I can probably make the grades. Yet, I don't know what I want to be. I feel that if I don't try for some hard goal God will be displeased with me by being a cop out and taking an easy course in life. I keep thinking about the parable of the talents where the one that had a few used them and made more but the one that buried his was left with none (if this is the right parable). What should I do?*

You have asked a difficult question. It is never easy to know exactly what God wants us to do in those areas where His Holy Word does not direct us. The matter of one's vocation is one of the areas in which you cannot find a definite answer in the Bible.

Some people would suggest that you seek or wait for a special revelation from God in this matter. However, you may have heard the old story about the man who thought he saw a revelation from God in the clouds. He thought he saw the letters "P. C." in the clouds. He was convinced that the message was "preach Christ," and so he enrolled at a theological seminary. However, he had a rough time academically and found the preparation and delivery of sermons very difficult. As the story goes, a kindly old professor at the seminary talked with the discouraged fellow. In conversation the professor suggested to the lad that "P. C." may have meant "plow corn" rather than "preach Christ." That helped the fellow. He withdrew from the seminary and went back to the farm. He became a successful farmer; he served the Lord and shared his faith in Christ as a layman. The point of this old story is that we fallible human beings are quite capable of misinterpreting even authentic special revelations.

Rather than seek or wait for special revelations from God, it would seem wiser for you to find and develop the talents you do have. In the parable you mentioned all of the men got one or more talents. There is no such thing as an untalented person. As talented (less, average, or more talented) people, we are obligated to do the best we can with what we have. The man who buried his talent got in trouble with the master when

he returned, because he had simply buried it (he did nothing with it). So you should not despair because you do not *now* know exactly in what vocation to best serve the Lord. He knows, and I am confident that He shows His people in many and varied ways, where He wants them to go.

It might also be helpful for you to get involved in some way with those things that you think might be possibilities for your vocation. You may find that something you thought would be worthwhile is something that really does not interest or challenge you. At the same time, you may find something to which you really had not given much thought is the very thing which turns you on. Experience is not something you get by just thinking about it. Experience is obtained in the doing.

I do not mean to suggest that you should not also seek the Lord's guidance in prayer. In prayer submit yourself to Him and let Him know the desires of your heart. Pray the prayer of Jesus in the Garden of Gethsemane: "Nevertheless not My will, but Thine, be done" (Luke 22:42). There *will* be an answer.

# Index of Bible Passages